DATA WAREHOUSES: MORE THAN JUST MINING

Barbara J. Bashein
California State University San Marcos

and

M. Lynne Markus
Claremont Graduate University

A publication of Financial Executives Research Foundation, Inc.

Financial Executives Research Foundation, Inc.
10 Madison Avenue
P.O. Box 1938
Morristown, NJ 07962-1938
(973) 898-4608

International Standard Book Number 1-885065-19-1
Library of Congress Catalog Card Number 99-76923
Printed in the United States of America

First Printing

Financial Executives Research Foundation, Inc. (FERF®) is the research affiliate of Financial Executives Institute. The basic purpose of the Foundation is to sponsor research and publish informative material in the field of business management, with particular emphasis on the practice of financial management and its evolving role in the management of business.

The views set forth in this publication are those of the authors and do not necessarily represent those of the FERF Board as a whole, individual trustees, or the members of the Advisory Committee.

FERF publications can be ordered by calling 1-800-680-FERF
(U.S. and Canada only; international orders, please call 770-751-1986).
Quantity discounts are available.

Cover design by Mark Tocchet

ADVISORY COMMITTEE

CONTENTS

FOREWORD

When Barbara Bashein and Lynne Markus first approached me about participating in a data warehouse study, I was eager to share my experiences. I expected the project to uncover helpful insights about the lessons that small to mid-sized companies can learn about implementing data warehousing from the large companies. A couple of months later when I met with Barbara and Lynne again, they joked about titling the research "What the large corporation can learn about data warehousing from the small guy."

Indeed, in this study you will discover that a data warehouse project does not necessarily require a large budget and years of effort. Modest investments in specific, divisional data mart projects can yield immediate returns and can provide an excellent foundation for a more encompassing, enterprise data warehouse implementation. Each of the companies interviewed for this study experienced an early payback in terms of improved internal efficiencies. Each also learned certain lessons:

It is hard to find good help. Finding the information technology (IT) talent necessary to write specialized reports in response to ad hoc queries is challenging. Each of the participants in this study implemented self-service reporting mechanisms on top of a data mart or warehouse. These projects generated valuable tools to meet the demand of instantaneous access to information by a wider population.

Growth drives industries. Every vibrant company, large or small, is looking for opportunities to grow its business. Responding to the increased data management demands caused by mergers and acquisitions puts additional strain on the IT support group. Capturing, assimilating, and making sense out of the data from disparate systems poses special challenges to a rapidly evolving company. Throughout this study, you will see how the participating companies used data warehouse techniques to give them a competitive advantage by turning data into useful knowledge.

Kraft Foods implemented several data marts as part of its strategy to effectively integrate data from dozens of legacy systems from acquisitions. MSC.Software implemented a revenue data mart to replace a family of slow, burdensome, incomplete revenue reports. Alaris Medical Systems demonstrated that an evolutionary approach can be used to meet the demand of specific, immediate self-service reporting needs, and can grow to meet the needs of a wider audience. Cardinal Health used a data warehouse as the foundation for its decision support system.

Although much of the research in this area has focused on the potential, long-term gains of data mining, Barbara and Lynne do an excellent job of identifying several immediate benefits that do not involve data mining. They demonstrate how a modest investment in data warehouse technologies can help companies manage information growth and can lay the groundwork for supporting future information exploration projects. The study describes how effective uses of data warehouse technologies produce targeted strategies that achieve tangible results.

Daniel Bryce
Chief Information Officer
MSC.Software

Introduction

Data mining is much in the news these days, portrayed as a panacea for corporate marketing departments. Articles in the business and trade press cite successes of companies that are mining customer data to uncover previously hidden revenue-generating opportunities, to create lasting customer relationships, or to achieve elusive mass-customization goals. Here are two of many examples:

- Farmers Group extracted revenue opportunities by challenging the conventional wisdom that drivers of high-performance sports cars are more likely to have accidents.[1] Through data mining, Farmers Group discovered that as long as the sports car wasn't the only vehicle in the household, the accident rate wasn't much greater than that of a regular car. Thus, by letting Corvettes and Porsches into its preferred premium plan, Farmers estimated it could bring in an additional $4.5 million in premiums without a significant rise in claims.

- NextCard used data mining to customize credit cards[2] because people with personalized cards are more likely to use them. Within seconds on a Web site, NextCard tailors multiple credit card offers (credit terms) to reflect potential customers' current account balances and credit bureau histories. Then, after customers select their personalized credit terms, NextCard offers them further customization—they can transmit their favorite photo (one customer chose a photo of an airplane he's building), which is included on the credit card.

These and other high-profile stories focus on mining customer data. What they don't explain is that data mining requires data warehousing: Before the data can be used, they must be assembled, cleaned, organized, and stored. The stories also don't say that many other types of data besides customer data can be effectively warehoused and used.

Because of these omissions, the publicity creates two misleading impressions—that data mining is the important focus and that data warehousing is primarily a marketing tool.

In this study, we found the reality to be different. On the positive side, we found many uses of data warehouses—less glamorous than data mining—that receive little publicity but achieve significant payoffs. Examples include reporting financial information, tracking product quality data, and consolidating travel and entertainment expenses. On the negative side, however, we found that data warehousing is not quick and easy—it's time consuming and difficult. Even companies with sophisticated information systems (IS) departments have to make significant investments in time, money, and human resources in order to build and use data warehouses effectively.

Why Did We Do This Study?

Our previous study[3] for the Financial Executives Research Foundation, Inc. (FERF®) highlights two innovative users of data warehousing. BankAmerica, a data warehousing pioneer, was enormously successful in achieving business value from mining customer data. Microsoft used data warehousing as part of a strategy for making financial data available electronically within the company (eliminating the distribution of paper reports) and for enabling do-it-yourself reporting on demand. Our previous study focused on the risks of technologies such as data warehousing, but FERF was also interested in the benefits. So we undertook the current study to analyze how companies were using this technology and achieving benefits from it.

Since a significant percentage of Financial Executives Institute (FEI) members represent small to medium-sized companies, FERF was particularly interested in how such companies could benefit from data warehousing. (BankAmerica and Microsoft are clearly not small, and they are also technology leaders.) So, we sought to learn about the uses, benefits, and difficulties of using this technology in smaller organizations.

Small and medium-sized companies are of particular interest for two reasons:

■ *Technology trends.* Technology vendors are introducing more scaleable data warehousing products that can accommodate small data marts and can grow to large-scale data warehouses. These new products—both hardware and software—are making the benefits of data warehousing available to organizations of all sizes—even those with limited resources in time and money.

■ *Organizational reporting structures.* In small and medium-sized companies, the IS function often reports to the CFO, who may need to initiate or oversee a data warehousing effort.

What Is the Focus of This Study?

This study focuses on a suite of related technologies and how they are used. One of these, data warehousing, is the enabling technology for data mining. But, as this report will show, its uses go far beyond data mining. Another relevant term is data mart, a variant on the data warehouse.

■ A *data warehouse* is an environment—not a single technology—comprising a data store and multiple software products often obtained from different vendors. The products include tools for data extraction, loading, storage, access, query, and reporting. The data store is a collection of subject-oriented, integrated, time-variant, nonvolatile data that is queried to support management decisionmaking. Data stores include immense volumes of information detailing every aspect of a particular subject (such as customers, suppliers, products, markets, or quality). This information is drawn from a company's internal operational systems (such as order entry, sales, accounting, manufacturing, and human resources systems) and from external sources (such as purchased market research and demographic data). Data warehouses are typically assembled to support decision-oriented management queries. Because frequent and/or sophisticated queries can slow operational systems, data warehouses are established and maintained apart from the production systems. Cross-indexed and supported by significant computing power, data are refreshed periodically and do not change with each query or access.

- A *data mart* is a collection of data and tools focused on a specific business unit or problem. Size does not distinguish data marts, but they tend to be smaller than data warehouses.

- *Data mining* is a collection of tools and techniques used for inductive rather than deductive analyses. Using sophisticated data mining tools, analysts explore detailed data and business transactions to uncover meaningful insights, relationships, trends, or patterns within the business activity and/or history. Data mining is used to identify hypotheses; traditional queries are used to test hypotheses.

What Are the Objectives of This Study?

With data warehousing and mining technologies becoming more affordable for smaller companies, many businesses are considering implementing them. These businesses need answers to some key questions. The objectives of this study are to answer these questions:

- How are companies, especially small and medium-sized companies, using the technologies of data warehousing and data mining?

- What kinds of benefits do users of data warehousing and mining achieve?

- How do organizational changes (e.g., pending mergers or acquisitions) complicate data warehouse implementation?

- How can businesses jump-start their efforts to use the technology and ensure that the technology delivers business value?

- How can businesses avoid the pitfalls of spending too much time and money, reproducing the same old databases, and getting inadequate paybacks?

- How can businesses develop realistic business cases to decide whether warehousing makes sense?

Our prior research also suggested that benefits from data warehousing depend not just on a sound business case and a good implementation plan but also on an orientation toward performance measurement and continuous learning or improvement. Without a management culture that measures and monitors performance and that demands and rewards improvement, the real gains of data warehousing will not be achieved. This, in turn, may require above-average information technology and data analysis skills among data warehouse users. Thus, this study examines the relationship between a learning orientation and data warehousing success and suggests what businesses can do to promote a performance orientation.

Why Is Data Warehousing Important?

Before undertaking this study, we knew that data warehousing technologies could provide big paybacks to large companies that were mining their data, as demonstrated by the successes of organizations such as BankAmerica, Frito-Lay, Microsoft, MCI Worldcom, and Wal-Mart. Capitalizing on their sophisticated IS departments, these organizations built and mined huge data warehouses to focus marketing programs, to identify and quantify risks, and to manage inventories effectively.

In this study we examine four cases in detail: two large companies and two medium-sized companies. (Large companies have annual revenues over $1 billion. This category includes all *Fortune* 1000.) We learned that data warehousing technologies can provide relatively big paybacks to smaller and medium-sized companies and to large companies composed of multiple acquisitions), and to companies not mining their data. While the uses of data warehousing technologies in many of these instances were relatively mundane (e.g., reporting financial information, tracking data on product quality, and consolidating travel and entertainment expenses), the paybacks were quicker and easier to achieve than the marketing-oriented data mining examples highlighted in the news. In this monograph, we describe effective uses of data warehousing technologies and effective strategies for achieving results.

How Is This Study Organized?

Chapter 2 describes the methods we followed in conducting this study. Chapter 3 outlines some initial findings from literature and early data collection activities. These initial findings guided our approach to the four case studies presented in chapters 4 through 7 (ALARIS Medical Systems, Kraft Foods, MSC.Software, and Cardinal Health). Chapter 8 summarizes findings from the case studies, and chapter 9 offers recommendations to organizations that plan to adopt and use these exciting information technologies. Appendix A is an annotated bibliography of publications on data warehousing, and appendix B is our research protocol. Appendix C is a glossary of terms used in this study.

Endnotes

1. Lisa Bransten. "Looking For Patterns." *The Wall Street Journal,* June 21, 1999, R16, R20.

2. Heather Green. "The Information Gold Mine." *Business Week E.Biz,* July 26, 1999, EB 17-30.

3. Barbara J. Bashein, M. Lynne Markus, and Jane B. Finley. *Safety Nets: Secrets of Effective Information Technology Controls.* Morristown, NJ: Financial Executives Research Foundation, Inc., 1997.

Approach and Methodology

In this study we addressed technical, business, and organizational issues related to data warehousing. To view data warehousing from these different perspectives, we employed multiple research methodologies, including telephone surveys and in-depth case studies. Using multiple methodologies, we were better able to verify, cross check, and substantiate our findings and recommendations.

Segments of the Study

We divided the study into the five segments described below. (Also see the Summary Work Plan.)

Literature Review

We began our project with a literature review. We studied print and electronic sources of information on data warehousing and related topics. The topics included technology issues, data warehousing uses and benefits, IT cost-benefit analyses, data warehouse implementation strategies and tactics, and organizational challenges. We revisited the literature review at several points throughout the project to make sure we kept up with current publications.

Our sources of literature included business publications (e.g., *The Wall Street Journal* and *Harvard Business Review*), academic books and journals (e.g., *Communications of the ACM* and *Information Systems Research*), practitioner publications (e.g., *CIO* and *CFO*), and trade publications (e.g., *Computerworld* and *Information Week*). The deliverable from this phase of the project was an annotated bibliography (see the appendix), which highlights some of the literature we reviewed over the course of this research project.

Vendor Reviews

We studied the products from leading vendors of data warehousing tools to summarize the costs and capabilities (without attributing specific costs or capabilities to particular vendors). We visited Web sites and read trade publications, product literature, white papers, and case studies. We paid particular attention to the learning aspects of data warehouse successes—lessons that could be generalized to businesses undertaking or contemplating data warehouse projects.

From these efforts we produced an interim set of questions to guide the next segments of the research. We developed these questions by analyzing information from the literature survey and the vendor reviews.

Company Survey

We surveyed 25 companies that either were implementing or had completed data warehouses. Our agreement with these companies was that they would remain anonymous, so the individuals we interviewed were willing to share their challenges, successes, failures, and lessons learned.

We conducted both telephone and in-person interviews with one or more representatives from each of the 25 companies. The companies represented a cross section of organizational sizes, industries, and data warehouse uses (e.g., customer data, financial data, human resources data, product data) and included some organizations for which information is a product. The interviews focused on the following:

- The history of data warehousing at the company, including the technologies and an overview of the experience.

- A summary of the costs, benefits, and unanticipated impacts and advice to others on how to build a sound business case for a data warehouse.

- Highlights of the implementation approach, including problems and strategies for coping with them.

- The learning aspects of organizational culture and their relationships to the data warehouse experience.

- Lessons learned and advice to others embarking on or engaged in data warehousing projects.

The product from this and previous phases of the project was the case-study protocol (see appendix B) that we used to conduct the next phase of the project. In addition, we identified survey companies that we would ask to participate as case studies in the next phase of the project. We selected four companies of different sizes and from different industries so that our case studies would be representative of FEI members. In addition, the companies were using their warehouses for different types of data, including customer, financial, quality, product, sales, and service.

Case Studies

We conducted in-depth case studies of the four companies—ALARIS Medical Systems, Cardinal Health, Kraft Foods, and MSC.Software. These companies reviewed the case-study protocol and agreed to participate as identified sites in our research study.

We spent several days on site at each study company. Before our visit to a company, we reviewed public information about the company, including annual reports, newspaper articles, and Web sites. During our visit, we conducted interviews, went on tours, sat in on meetings, observed operations, reviewed materials, and watched demonstrations. We analyzed each case independently before completing the cross-case analyses in the next segment.

Analysis, Synthesis, and Monograph Preparation

We analyzed, synthesized, and integrated the results across the four case-study companies and across all previous segments of the project to prepare the final monograph.

Organization of this Report

The remaining chapters are organized as follows:

- *Chapter 3: Highlights of the Literature and the Survey.* This chapter summarizes our findings from the literature survey, the vendor reviews, and the company survey.

- *Chapters 4 through 7: Case Studies.* These chapters tell the data warehousing stories of our four case-study sites. Rather than presenting these companies in alphabetical order, we chose to arrange the chapters according to the companies' uses of data warehousing. The first three companies—ALARIS Medical Systems, Kraft Foods, and MSC.Software—used their warehouses to satisfy reporting and systems integration needs. The fourth company—Cardinal Health—used its warehouse for reporting, systems integration, and new data products.

- *Chapter 8: Lessons Learned.* This chapter summarizes the findings from the four case studies and highlights where and how our findings differ from previous literature.

- *Chapter 9: Recommendations.* This chapter includes specific recommendations that executives and managers who are building or planning to build data warehouses can take back to their companies. These recommendations are based on our analysis and synthesis across all segments of the study—our literature review, our vendor reviews, our company survey, and our case studies.

Table 2.1
Summary Work Plan

Major Tasks	Key Deliverables
Literature review	Appendix A—Anno-tated bibliography
1. Identify sources of relevant print and electronic literature	
2. Review sources for pertinent articles	
3. Analyze and synthesize findings from the literature	
4. Draft annotated bibliography	
Vendor reviews	Interim set of ques-tions to guide the next segments of the study
1. Identify key vendors	
2. Locate material on capabilities, costs, etc.	
3. Review and analyze vendor material	
4. Synthesize information from literature/vendor reviews	
5. Develop questions for the next phases of the research	
Company survey	Chapter 3—Highlights of the Literature and the Survey
1. Identify survey participants	
2. Prepare interview questionnaires	
3. Schedule and conduct interviews	Appendix B—Case-study protocol
4. Review, analyze, and synthesize results of interviews	
5. Develop case-study protocol	
6. Identify study sites and secure approval for participation	
Case studies	Chapters 4, 5, 6, and 7—Case-study write-ups
1. Obtain and review background materials on each study site	
2. Identify individuals at each site for interviews	
3. Arrange/schedule site visits and interviews	
4. Conduct site visits and interviews	
5. Perform within-case analysis for each case	
6. Follow up with participants on any open questions	
7. Draft case-study write-ups	
8. Review drafts with participants	
9. Revise drafts as needed	
Analysis, synthesis, and monograph preparation	Chapter 8—Lessons Learned
1. Perform cross-case analysis among the four case studies	
2. Analyze, synthesize, and integrate results across all previous segments	Chapter 9—Recommendations
3. Identify key findings and recommendations	Final manuscript
4. Develop draft of full monograph	
5. Revise draft as needed and prepare monograph for publication	

Highlights of the Literature and the Survey

The term "data warehousing" is something of a misnomer. It implies that the main problem is one of *storing* data. In fact, however, the important issue is *using* data—accessing, retrieving, and analyzing them. When the emphasis is on using data, the terms "decision support" or (more recently) "data mining" are used. Decision support refers to information technology intended to influence how people make decisions[1]; decision support systems generally involve databases, analysis tools, and models that represent a problem situation or analytic strategy. "Data mining" (called "knowledge discovery in databases" in academic circles) uses a variety of inductive techniques such as artificial intelligence to find patterns in large datasets.

While most of the business value comes from the use of data rather than just its storage, data warehousing is important as an *enabling* technology: Data warehousing is generally regarded today as the prerequisite for effective decision support or data mining. Data warehousing helps organizations get value from data they already have, locked away in transaction processing systems (or available for purchase from outside sources), but cannot easily access.

Decision support is not a new concept. One of the earliest concerns of the discipline of management information systems was summarizing and reporting the data from an organization's basic record-keeping systems (called transaction processing systems) to help managers control operations. Gradually, the emphasis shifted toward more sophisticated models and analyses for allocating scarce resources (e.g., locating plants and warehouses, managing cash flow, planning advertising budgets) and strategic decisionmaking (e.g., capital investment decisions). Until recently, however, decision support systems rarely lived up to their promise. Limited computer processing power, poor software development tools, and traditional programming practices (such as developing nonintegrated, functionally oriented applications) have made it difficult for organizations to analyze data in ways that were not anticipated and programmed in advance. Consider this example:

> The personal computers in the Office of Development [at Yale University in New Haven, Conn.] had no way of directly accessing the Oracle databases that resided on an IBM RS/6000 four-processor server in the university's data center. Fund-raisers had to write detailed requests on slips of paper, which guided administrative assistants in querying the database. Then they often had to wait 24 hours for the reports to be delivered.[2]

Early executive information systems (EISs), precursors of data warehousing, often exhibited tradeoffs between ease of use and analytic power. A great deal of human intervention was required to extract data from operational databases and produce customized data displays. Lacking easy-to-use analysis tools, executives had to be content with preprogrammed ("canned") management reports.

The difference today is that tools and methodologies exist to provide the long-envisioned capability of decision support. Further, today's technologies enable analyses of very large databases (multi-terabytes) both with statistical methods and with a variety of "knowledge discovery" tools, such as artificial intelligence and neural networks (networks that learn through pattern matching and the equivalent of behavioral reinforcement). The latter capabilities go well beyond traditional "exception reporting"; they provide the ability to "mine" data for previously unknown relationships. (The classic example of unknown relationships is the apocryphal "diapers and beer" relationship from retailing: Young fathers often purchase beer when they run out to buy their babies' disposable diapers.[3])

So, what's new is that the tools for decision support and knowledge discovery are finally useful. But they are not necessarily cheap or easy to use. In our review of the literature and conversations with people in organizations that did not become case-study sites, we identified many challenges facing organizations that want to adopt the technologies of data warehousing. We discuss these challenges below in three categories:

1. Challenges relating to the technology of data warehousing and how that technology is acquired and put to use.

2. Challenges relating to the data required for data warehousing and its uses.

3. Challenges relating to organizational issues.

As an introduction to the discussion of these challenges, however, it is useful to have a broad understanding of how organizations go about building data warehouses.

Building Data Warehouses

The literature on data warehousing suggests three broad approaches to building data warehouses. We call them the enterprise solution approach, the evolutionary approach, and the package approach.

Enterprise Solution Approach

When experts first began promoting the data warehousing concept in the late 1980s, they described the technology as an enterprise-wide repository of key organizational data. Because most organizations at that time had a patchwork of unintegrated systems with redundant and missing data, it was believed that organizations should first undertake a "strategic data planning effort" to define key business concepts and data analysis needs. (Worldwide operations and corporate acquisitions make the issues of patchwork systems more prevalent in today's business environment.) When the data planning effort was complete, organizations would design an architecture for the data warehouse and populate it with data. (The latter step might require extensive data cleaning and conversion activities.) Subsequently, the organization might develop specialized, subject-oriented data marts (e.g., a customer service data mart or a quality data mart) to facilitate efficient response to users' queries.

Industry experience with strategic data planning was not good. People complained that the process cost too much, took too long, and produced highly abstract results. Technical specialists had difficulty securing participation of knowledgeable businesspeople; when participation was good, it was often difficult to obtain consensus on the key data elements and their definitions. (One classic example concerns the meaning of a "sale." Is a sale defined as the point when the customer tells a salesperson "I want one," when accounts receivable does a credit check and processes a deposit, when the legal department has a signed contract, etc.?)

Today, observers have begun to question the need for strategic data planning as a foundation for data warehousing and its uses. They argue that a single data model should adequately serve most organizations in an industry; few organizations in an industry have unique data needs. (The same logic has helped fuel the widespread adoption of enterprise systems.) Consultants have begun developing industry-specific data models as the basis of some of the subject-oriented packaged data warehousing solutions discussed later.

An additional wrinkle in the enterprise solution approach seems to be that different kinds of data and decision problems lend themselves to different data warehousing tools and techniques. It simply may not be possible to design a grand architecture that works well for all parts of the business. Many experts still believe that the enterprise solution is best. But a number of organizations have taken the more pragmatic approach of building one data mart at a time and worrying about the enterprise solution later.

Evolutionary Approach

A fair number of companies (including all our case-study sites) take the pragmatic approach of building data marts to deal with specific subject-oriented business needs. An example is customer prospecting or product-quality analysis. In the ideal version of this strategy, a company would populate a corporate data warehouse with data from a variety of data marts.

A recognized hazard of this approach is that companies can wind up with a proliferation of marts with different standards, technologies, and data definitions—in short, a quagmire of nonintegration and maintenance hassles similar to the situation that led to the pursuit of data warehousing in the first place. The challenge is to make progress solving immediate business needs while developing a flexible overall architecture to guide future data warehousing developments. For reasons involving the technology, data characteristics, and organizational issues, this is not an easy tradeoff to manage.

The Package Approach

An emerging approach is package solutions for data warehousing. One type of package is offered by the vendors of enterprise software products, such as SAP, Baan, Peoplesoft, and Oracle. These packages are specifically designed to work with the vendors' operational databases. Another type is subject-oriented packages for a particular industry, usually developed by systems consulting firms such as KPMG or IBM. (These companies also supply components for customers to integrate themselves.) Examples include data warehouses for customer retention in financial services or preventing fraud in the insurance business.

To date there has been little experience with such packages. Some observers express concerns about how well packages developed for specific enterprise systems will accommodate data from legacy systems or purchased external data. The jury is still out on these packaged solutions. Most organizations are still building their own data warehouses from components, using either the enterprise solution or the evolutionary approach.

Technical and Sourcing Challenges

According to both the literature and our initial company interviews, building and using data warehouses successfully are difficult for a number of reasons related to the current state of the technology and to the vendors that supply it. Among the challenges are the following:

■ *Numerous technical options.* Data warehouses consist of tools for extracting, storing, accessing, and analyzing data from a variety of in-house and external sources. For each stage in data warehousing, numerous options exist. An organization can, for example, select ROLAP or MOLAP (relational or multidimensional options for online analytical processing). It can use a star schema or a snowflake schema for data modeling. Particular options may be available only from certain vendors. It is not always clear which option best fits the data or business problem. Figure 3.1 (reproduced from a technical publication) gives a hint of the technical complexity of data warehousing projects. The chart represents the processes and related products that assist in the successful im-

Figure 3.1
Atre's Data Warehouse/Data Mart Navigator™

©Copyright 1997–2000 by Atre Group, Inc. www.atre.com

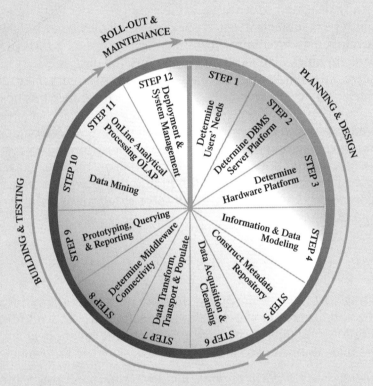

©Copyright 1997–2000 by Atre Group, Inc. www. atre.com

STEP 1: DETERMINE USERS' NEEDS
Do we need a data warehouse or even a data mart?
- What are the business objectives?
- Where do we get the data from?
- Cost/benefit analysis, project estimation & risk assessment.

STEP 2: DETERMINE DBMS SERVER PLATFORM
- Which database servers do we already have?
- Cost, interoperability, staff training considerations.
- Determine DBMS server platform based on ROI.

STEP 3: DETERMINE HARDWARE PLATFORM
Where should the data warehouse/data mart be housed?
- Which hardware platforms do we already have and/or use?
- Cost, interoperability, staff training considerations.
- Determine hardware based on ROI.

Figure 3.1, continued
Atre's Data Warehouse/Data Mart Navigator™

©Copyright 1997–2000 by Atre Group, Inc. www.atre.com

STEP 4: INFORMATION & DATA MODELING
Building an information model.
- How do we express relationships between the data with a data model?
- Access & usage issues.
- Logical & physical design of the data warehouse/data mart.

STEP 5: CONSTRUCT METADATA REPOSITORY
Keeping track of what means what, who can access it, and how it can be accessed.
- Building a metadata repository.
- Business user's view of metadata.
- Steps to develop an effective metadata repository.

STEP 6: DATA ACQUISITION & CLEANSING
How do we...
- Extract
- Cleanse
- Summarize
- Scrub
- Reconcile
- Aggregate
...data from various sources for the data warehouse/data mart?

STEP 7: DATA TRANSFORM, TRANSPORT & POPULATE
How do we build the data warehouse/data mart by:
- Transforming the data.
- Transporting the data.
- Populating the data warehouse/data mart.

STEP 8: DETERMINE MIDDLEWARE CONNECTIVITY
How do we connect the source data to the target data warehouse/data mart with:
- Ongoing connection?
- Direct data access?

STEP 9: PROTOTYPING, QUERYING & REPORTING
How do we:
- Implement a prototype with user involvement?
- Develop applications?
- Use querying & reporting tools?

STEP 10: DATA MINING
- How do we find data patterns in our data warehouse/data mart?
- How do we recognize the patterns for revenue growth?
- How do we use the tools to further identify patterns in the data?

STEP 11: ONLINE ANALYTICAL PROCESSING (OLAP)
- How can our users analyze the data?
- How can they see the data presented in multiple dimensions?
- Determining the number of dimensions to be effective.
- How can our users implement the OLAP tools?

STEP 12: DEPLOYMENT & SYSTEM MANAGEMENT
Providing security, backup, recovery & necessary capabilities of a production data warehouse/data mart.
- Allocating the resources.
- Accommodating growth of data.
- Keeping everything running smoothly.

plementation of a data warehouse. The details of this chart are now somewhat out of date, but the general message should be clear: Successful data warehousing requires many skills, including the very important skills of managing complex projects.

- *Rapidly developing technology and vendor shakeout.* Data warehousing technology is changing rapidly, and a consolidation of vendors and products is under way. Consequently, it is common for organizations to place their bets on technologies that soon become obsolete. The result can be maintenance headaches or a dizzying and costly cycle of upgrades and conversions.

- *Integration needs.* Different data warehousing components acquired from different vendors need to be integrated with one another and with the organization's data. One interviewee likened the process to "building a Swiss watch—it's got lots of moving parts." Not all products work well with each other, even if they are sold by the same vendor. (In the ongoing shakeout of data warehousing vendors, many data warehousing products have been acquired from their original developers and packaged with other products as an integrated product suite.) We were told of cases in which version 3 of a vendor's X tool would work only with version 4 of the vendor's Y tool, but version 4 had yet to be released!

- *Expertise gaps and knowledge transfer problems.* Because the technologies are so new and demand for skilled personnel is so high, it is hard for organizations to attract knowledgeable personnel and to retain those personnel once they are experienced. Expertise gaps are especially likely in smaller organizations. In some cases, the skills shortages extend to vendor consulting personnel. One interviewee described being assigned "experienced" consulting personnel who were trained only on an earlier version of the product being implemented.

Data Challenges

A second set of challenges concerns the data required to populate the data warehouse. Among the data challenges mentioned in the literature and our initial interviews are the following:

- *Uncertain information requirements.* It is generally acknowledged that determining requirements for decision support systems is more challenging than for transaction processing systems. Methods of performing a requirements analysis that work for traditional systems do not work well for unstructured decision support problems. Developers we interviewed described much difficulty determining users' requirements and noted that turnover of users sometimes required major changes in a warehouse's data structures. One interviewee noted that external consultants were not as good as internal IT specialists at challenging potential users' data requirements and reducing them to a manageable list. There is no generally accepted methodology for determining the information requirements for a data warehouse. (And, indeed, at ALARIS, data warehouse developers found users' stated requirements confusing and misleading; they ultimately relied on logic to create a working prototype, which they refined over time with users' feedback.)

- *Historical data requirements.* Some organizations are required to maintain large volumes of data about their customers, products, product service histories, etc., for a very long time. For example, a manufacturer of industrial pumps had to keep records on installed products for the life of the installations—often 20 years or more. Manufacturers of drugs and medical products must keep detailed product tracking records at the level of individual items sold.

- *Data quality.* IT changes rapidly, as do data storage media and formatting conventions. Because data warehouses assemble data from multiple sources, many different conversion routines may be required to render data in the format required by the warehouse. Further, the quality of data in old legacy systems is notoriously poor. Over time, users may have stopped entering data in particular fields or may have begun entering textual comments in fields intended for numeric input. Human knowledge can often fill in the gaps in traditional record-keeping systems, but the intended uses of data warehouses demand high-quality data.[4]

■ *Data naming and defining.* Historically, the transaction processing systems that supply many of the data for data warehouses have been built to support individual functional areas, such as sales or production. Most data warehouses require data from at least two functional areas (c.g., sales and accounting). When data warehouses are constructed, it is often found that systems in different functional areas employ similar concepts but define them differently or collect and compute data about them on different schedules. Recall our earlier example of confusion about the meaning of a "sale." One organization told us it had many different definitions of "full-time equivalent personnel"; another couldn't resolve the question, "how many days are there in a month?" Consequently, the answer to a query—and what that answer means—may depend on the source. A large part of data warehousing construction is obtaining consensus on the appropriate sources and definitions of various data elements.

■ *Data availability.* In some cases, the organization may not currently have the data required to answer important business questions. If the data are not collected by the source systems, or if the source systems are not properly integrated, it may not be possible to get the desired response, regardless of the analytic power in the data warehouse. Therefore, in some cases, solving business problems may require changing the source data collection and processing systems in addition to developing a data warehouse. The need to do so substantially increases project cost and risk.

Experts say that the "data" piece of a data warehousing project accounts for the largest part—upwards of 70 percent—of project time and expense. Political problems, discussed below, exacerbate the challenges of data naming, cleaning, and conversion.

Organizational Challenges

The literature and our initial interviews suggest a sizable number of organizational challenges to the successful development and use of data warehouses. Among them are the following:

■ *Cross-functional project leadership.* Even subject-oriented data marts usually cross the boundaries between two or more functional areas or business units. Consequently, the leadership of data warehousing projects is often a matter of contention—where several units vie for control, or abdication—where no one wants to assume responsibility for achieving a successful outcome. For example, one interviewee explained that his organization experienced difficulty getting executive support for investing in data warehousing because executives never experienced personal difficulty getting the reports they wanted. (But their analysts suffered endless hassles while preparing the reports.) Further, having someone assume project leadership is no guarantee of technical expertise sufficient to oversee important project decisions. (This challenge may be lower in smaller organizations, owing to fewer organizational units and to the strong role of chief financial officers in IT decisionmaking.)

■ *IT politics.* In larger organizations, responsibility for IT is usually segmented into infrastructure (corporate) versus applications (business units or departments). Data warehousing cannot be assigned unambiguously to either of these classifications. Since many data warehouses are subject oriented and concern the "application" of decision support, they can justifiably be claimed by the applications side of the IT shop. But since data warehousing concerns integration across the enterprise and applications development standards (another "corporate" responsibility), it can also be legitimately claimed by the infrastructure side of the IT shop. Conflict over data warehousing among IT personnel may exacerbate the difficulty of developing successful data warehouses.

■ *Organizational politics.* Data warehousing is first and foremost a scheme for integrating data from various sources into a single shared source for analysis. Few information-related issues are more contentious in organizations than common systems and data sharing. Subunit department heads often fiercely defend their desires for systems tailored to their specific needs. How else will their managers be able to achieve subunit goals? Data sharing raises the specter of interference from above and invidious comparisons with one's peers. The politics of information can derail even well-conceived data warehousing projects. Even when the data warehousing project is successfully completed, use of the data warehouse depends absolutely on subunits' trust in the accuracy of the data. Leaders of successful data warehousing initiatives in complex organizations need to be skilled in managing organizational politics and change. A useful tactic is to make public demonstrations of the warehouse's data quality. (Several of our case study sites used this tactic.)

■ *Human factors.* A goal in many data warehousing initiatives is to expand the population of users and/or their analytic skills. Many managerial and technical personnel today are quite happy to rely on others to perform analyses for them. Training in new tools alone may not be enough to move people from nonuse or underuse to effective and innovative use of data analysis tools. Research evidence shows that managers object to using models in decisionmaking. An interviewee from a consumer products firm that successfully mined internal and external data explained that he was trying to "make marketing types into scientific managers."

> I teach them one at a time by working with them in their own language. I never say to them "I'm teaching you regression analysis," but that's in effect what I'm doing.

Literature on data mining suggests that in addition to familiar hypothesis testing (deductive) analysis, managers need to be taught knowledge discovery (inductive) processes. End-user skill development is particularly essential for data mining because spurious results can lead to major negative consequences for the organization.

■ *Data privacy.* Many potentially valuable secondary uses of an organization's transaction data involve some perceived threats to customer or employee privacy. We covered this issue at some length in our prior FERF monograph.[5] Suffice it to say here that concerns about authorized use or perceived unauthorized use of data about customers and others is a barrier to the use of data warehousing in some organizations.

■ *Managing expectations.* A consistent theme in our interviews with technical specialists involved in data warehousing initiatives was the need for, and difficulty of, managing executive expectations about the technology. It often takes hard selling to convince senior executives to invest in data warehousing (an infrastructure investment with non-obvious or intangible payoffs), but it's easy to oversell them on the benefits and the timing of benefits. With a technology still under development and benefits requiring organizational change and learning, data warehousing is often best viewed as organizational research and development.

See table 3.1 for a summary of the technical, data, and organizational challenges in the effective implementation and use of data warehousing.

Summary

Our review of the literature on data warehousing and related topics and our initial interviews with companies that did not become case-study sites reveal that data warehousing is currently a poorly understood technology. Barriers to the successful development and use of data warehousing arise from the base technologies of data warehousing and their vendors, from the data that are warehoused and analyzed, and from the organization in which the data warehouse is deployed. The challenges concern technical personnel (both inside and outside the organization), the intended end-users of the technology, the managers responsible for funding, and the functional areas covered by the data warehouse.

The next four chapters present the four new case studies of data warehousing that we conducted for this report. The cases are ALARIS, Kraft Foods, MSC.Software, and Cardinal Health. However, in our prior FERF-sponsored study of the risks of large IT projects, two of the cases also involved data warehousing. Comparing those cases with the four new ones is instructive. Therefore, before presenting our new

Table 3.1
Data Warehousing Challenges

Category	Challenge	Description
Technical and Sourcing Challenges	Numerous technical options	Data warehousing consists of a set of tools for different purposes (e.g., storing versus analyzing data). Competing products, often with different technical options, exist within the same tool class. It is not always clear which option is best for a particular class of problems.
	Rapidly developing technology and vendor shakeout	Consolidation of available products is occurring. Some products and vendors are disappearing from the marketplace. Other vendors are assembling more complete product lines. Upgrades are frequent. Customers battle rapid obsolescence.
	Integration needs	Complete solutions may require integrating tools from different vendors.
	Expertise gaps and knowledge transfer problems	Skills in the core technologies of data warehousing are still quite scarce. Skills in integration are even scarcer. Acquiring and retaining skilled people is difficult for many companies.
Data Challenges	Uncertain information requirements	Requirements for data warehouses often cannot be clearly defined in advance of development. Iterative development strategies are often necessary for successful development.
	Historical data requirements	Some organizations must maintain records for many years. Cleaning, converting, and loading large amounts of historical data are onerous.
	Data quality	The quality of data in legacy systems and data stores is notoriously poor, necessitating lengthy and costly cleanup efforts.
	Data naming and defining	Organizations may assign many names to the same thing or may have many definitions for the same term. Effective data warehousing requires a certain degree of consensus on names and definitions.
	Data availability	Data needed for business decisionmaking may not currently exist in the company. It must be purchased externally or newly gathered.

Table 3.1
Data Warehousing Challenges

Category	Challenge	Description
Organizational Challenges	Cross-functional project leadership	Most data warehouses involve two or more organizational units as data owners or users. Jurisdictional disputes are common.
	IT politics	Data warehousing can be considered part of IT infrastructure or an IT application. In many organizations, infrastructure and applications are handled by different IT units. Jurisdictional disputes are common.
	Organizational politics	Organizational units may resist other units having access to their data. Data accessibility can create pressures for accountability and other types of organizational friction.
	Human factors	People may lack the skills to use the data warehouse effectively. They may not see the need to change their decision-making strategies. Poorly trained users create the risks of erroneous analyses or incorrect interpretations.
	Data privacy	When data about employees or customers is warehoused, concerns about privacy and access controls inevitably arise.
	Managing expectations	Data warehousing projects are hard to sell on the one hand and easily oversold on the other. Balancing expectations can be difficult.

cases, we briefly summarize the uses of data warehousing at BankAmerica and Microsoft.

Data Warehousing at BankAmerica—Summary

BankAmerica had long felt the need for a technology like data warehousing. Two prior attempts to develop data warehousing capability had failed. In the early 1980s, an attempt was made to provide decision support capability using the magnetic tape storage technology available then. The technology was unwieldy at best: A single query about marketing relationships using data from multiple operational systems required over 1,000 data tapes and 30 days to complete the processing. A second attempt several years later using hierarchical data structures and magnetic disk storage technology also failed. In 1986, the IT group in BankAmerica piloted the use of the Teradata® mass data storage system in the credit card accounts area, and the company's data warehousing success had begun.

Today, after 10 years of experience and evolution, BankAmerica considers data warehousing a mature technology. In 1987, the warehouse had 10 queries per day at an average cost of $2,430 per query; in 1997, it had 3,000 queries a day at an average cost of $18 each. The warehouse has grown to over 1.8 terabytes (trillion characters) of data about retail and wholesale customers. And use of the data warehouse has expanded to business units throughout the bank.

The data warehouse effort received a big push from 1989 to 1992, when the bank made 33 acquisitions, mainly failed savings and loan companies. The government made the failed banks' operational data available on tape to potential acquirers. BankAmerica loaded the data into a warehouse and analyzed them in comparison with data about the bank's own customers to determine the financial value to BankAmerica of the proposed acquisitions. It subsequently used the same method to analyze the acquisitions of Security Pacific Bank and Continental Bank. As a result of these experiences, bank officers became interested in analyzing the profitability of existing and new customers targeted with marketing initiatives. Today, data warehousing is recognized as a key strategic initiative of the bank.

The data in BankAmerica's warehouse come from both internal operational systems and external data providers (e.g., demographic data). The data are considered extremely sensitive, both from the perspective of corporate security (confidential competitive information) and from the perspective of customer privacy. Therefore, extensive efforts are made to safeguard this IT resource. Further, the bank recognizes that business losses may follow from unintended misuse of the system. Therefore, great effort is expended in maintaining metadata (data about the data elements stored in the warehouse) and in training users. Basic training in use of the warehouse takes four days (most of which is devoted to understanding the data); people who want to become "power users" of the warehouse undertake a six-month apprenticeship.

Data warehousing at BankAmerica can best be described as supporting the secondary use—or mining—of corporate and external data.

Data Warehousing at Microsoft—Summary

One use of data warehousing at Microsoft is to stage internal financial data and reports for access via the corporate intranet. In 1994, the Finance Group in Microsoft initiated a project to implement SAP R/3 financials worldwide with a common chart of accounts, replacing the diverse accounting systems used in about 60 subsidiaries. (This effort followed two failed attempts to implement SAP at Microsoft.) The key objective of the project was to get the Finance Group out of the business of producing financial reports. At that time, the month-end financial close took two weeks. Finance produced (printed, sorted, and mailed) approximately 350,000 paper financial reports a year, and specialized report requests often required specialists to rekey data from printed reports into custom Excel spreadsheets. Bill Gates' vision for IT is "information at everyone's fingertips"; similarly, Finance adopted the financial publishing vision of "do-it-yourself, print-on-demand reporting."

SAP R/3 was one step toward achieving that vision: The integrated package brought together the company's financial records and vastly streamlined the process of financial consolidation. But there still remained the task of producing and distributing financial reports. SAP's reporting software was thought to be not easy to use; Microsoft associates were unlikely to accept using this reporting tool. So the Finance Group decided to handle reporting by extracting data from the SAP operational databases and loading the data into a warehouse that could be queried with user-friendly access and reporting tools. It was decided to make the company's intranet the distribution medium for financial data. Password-authorized users could retrieve preformatted financial reports directly from the intranet. Users with legitimate needs for special ad hoc analyses could obtain access from registered data owners and use Microsoft's own products (Excel pivot tables) to construct their own reports.

This use of data warehousing at Microsoft can best be described as directed at the company's reporting needs.

Endnotes

1. Mark Silver. *Systems That Support Decision Makers: Description and Analysis.* Chichester: Wiley, 1991.

2. Peter Rubin. "Emerging Technology: Self-Service Information Retrieval." *CIO Magazine* March 15, 1999: www.cio.com/archive/031599_et_content.html.

3. Efraim Turban, noted textbook author, tells us the famous diapers-beer story is false.

4. The chart is Atre's Road Map for Data Warehouse/Data Mart implementation. Complimentary copies of the full-sized chart are available at http://www.atre.com.

5. In traditional record-keeping systems, there is much less "distance" (physical, temporal, organizational) between the collection of data and their use than there is in data warehousing.

6. Bashein, et al. *Safety Nets,* 1997.

ALARIS Medical Systems, Inc.

Company Profile

ALARIS Medical Systems develops, markets, and distributes products for the North American and international health care markets.[1] Headquartered in San Diego, the company distributes its products to more than 5,000 hospitals and alternate site providers in more than 120 countries worldwide. ALARIS Medical holds more than 200 unexpired patents in the United States and 400 unexpired patents in foreign countries, principally in Australia, Canada, Europe, and Japan.

ALARIS Medical is a pioneer in the development of intravenous (IV) infusion systems and patient monitoring. The company designs, manufactures, and markets IV infusion therapy products, patient monitoring instruments, and related disposable products, including cardiac event recorder and pacemaker follow-up systems. With annual sales (for the year ending December 31, 1999) of $402 million, ALARIS Medical is a leading provider of products in four categories:

- *Drug infusion systems,* including large-volume infusion systems, syringe pump infusion systems, and ambulatory pump infusion systems. ALARIS Medical is known for its IMED® and IVAC® brand names of intravenous infusion therapy systems.[2]

- *Patient monitoring systems,* including products that measure and monitor temperature, pulse, pulse oximetry, and blood pressure.

- *Cardiac telemedicine systems,* including arrhythmia-event recorders and pacemaker monitors for the alternate site market. ALARIS Medical is known for its Instromedix® cardiac event recorders and pacemaker follow-up systems.

■ *Specialty disposables,* including needle-free IV systems and IV administration sets.

The health care industry faces significant challenges: regulatory oversight by the U.S. Food and Drug Administration (FDA) and competing marketplace demands resulting from the trends in managed care. These demands include the following:

■ Cost—increasing pressures to maintain and even reduce costs.

■ Safety—growing concerns about caregiver and patient safety.

■ Quality—demands to improve the quality of patient care.

With these three demands setting the stage in the health care industry, the need is growing for medical devices that improve patient and caregiver safety, reduce medication errors, and provide enhanced data management. The estimated billion-dollar demand for technology solutions to safety issues confronting health care professionals is driven by medication errors (the fourth leading cause of death in the United States), which are responsible for significant health care costs. ALARIS Medical's products address the three demands of cost, safety, and quality by providing cost-effective solutions to key safety and quality issues—medication errors, caregiver safety, and IV site complications.

Senior management at ALARIS Medical has established a business goal of significant sales growth over the next several years. To meet this goal, ALARIS Medical is supplementing internal growth with acquisitions and alliances focused on the integration of infusion therapy, patient monitoring, and advanced data communications and data management. The acquisition of Instromedix, provider of arrhythmia-event recorders and pacemaker monitors, is an example of the implementation of this strategy. This business goal and associated acquisition strategy guided the direction of the data warehouse.

History of the Data Warehouse

The data warehouse initiative at ALARIS Medical dates to 1993. Analysts in Marketing, Sales, and Customer Service wanted customized reports—mostly sales information regarding specific products, customers, and/or dates.

The information resided in an old database. To access the information, analysts had to use Eztrieve, a tool that they found difficult and cumbersome. A few "super" users throughout the company developed customized reports with the tool. But the reports had to be run "as is" because they were too difficult to modify. If someone requested a change to a report and the analyst who had developed the original report had moved to another area of the company, the request had to be sent to the IS Department, where it was fielded by a "run the business" (RTB) support group. RTB included a staff of 10 analysts, who were overwhelmed trying to support reporting and other system requests.

As the demands for reporting continued to grow, the IS Department formed an Emerging Technologies (ET) group to look at alternative ways to satisfy the ever-increasing needs. Resources in the IS Department were stretched thin.

The ET group, which included representatives from outside the IS Department, assessed the needs and decided to investigate data warehousing alternatives and technologies. ET team members read data warehouse literature and attended seminars. They developed a preliminary design and presented the design to the "customer." (Members of the IS Department always refer to the user community as customers.) Paul Trivino, Principal Information Engineer, commented on the design process:

> Everything we did was by committee—focus groups, brainstorming, etc. I'm basically a propeller head, but the committee process worked. It was good timing. We had eight to 10 people—one representative from each major area. When we designed it, they understood it. The ones who got involved wanted to.

After several iterations of the design, the IS Department built and populated a prototype data warehouse on a Sequel server, using Business Objects as a query and reporting tool. A "proof of concept" period followed. During this period, senior people from Sales Operations who had been trained on the data and the Business Objects tool used the prototype, and they liked it. They liked it so much that the evaluation period lasted only two to three months. The warehouse was implemented and rolled out in December 1993.

As the level of use grew, the Sequel server bogged down. The IS Department decided to port the same design to an Oracle database, which it did by April 1994. At this point, the warehouse consisted of internal sales information extracted monthly from the legacy systems.

John Scholl, Manager of Business Support Systems, reflected back that the IS Department "didn't actively promote it [the warehouse] as much as we should have. We were worried about the size of the server." But it turned out that they didn't have to promote it—word of mouth was sufficient. The warehouse gained momentum. The Manufacturing group, for example, heard about the warehouse and wanted service and repair data added. The IS Department responded to these types of requests, and by the end of 1994, the warehouse had grown by 50 percent.

Then the IS Department formed a Data Resource Management Team. The team conducted monthly data warehouse training classes and published a newsletter, *The Data Warehouse News.* By 1995, 30 to 35 people were using the warehouse regularly and depended on it. So, the warehouse had to be both accessible and accurate. John Scholl emphasized that data accuracy and the ability to prove it were critical.

> One of the things we did right was to spend time on the integrity of the data. We made sure we could reconcile with Finance back to the general ledger. If there was a reporting error, we'd go back to the data and prove the accuracy. Sometimes we analyzed the query and traced the error back to the way the information was requested.

Evolution of the Data Warehouse

Since the inception of the warehouse, the structure and format of the data have been changed four times. New subject areas and new user groups have been added.

By the beginning of 1996, the original data warehouse had grown in both depth and breadth. In depth, the warehouse had been expanded to include both detailed and summary information. In breadth, the warehouse had been expanded to include numerous categories of internal information (e.g., agreements, buying groups, customers, installed instrument base, products, sales, and territories) as well as some purchased external data (e.g., hospital demographics).

More recently, other new subject areas were added to support FDA reporting and ISO 9000 efforts. These new subject areas included production-line defect information and materials-defect information (named NCMR for non-conforming material report).

The number of business units using the warehouse also grew. Sales Operations, Finance (both domestic and international), Marketing, Pricing, and Customer Service regularly used the sales data in the warehouse. When quality data were added to the warehouse, Service Repair, Manufacturing Operations, and Quality Control began using the warehouse regularly, too.

Expansion Opportunities

As the data warehouse became an increasingly valuable tool for decision support, ideas for expanding it emerged. Early in 1996, John Scholl and a colleague spent about a month evaluating expansion opportunities for the data warehouse. Their report, "The Data Warehouse: An Evaluation of Expansion Opportunities, 5/21/96," systematically presented several avenues for expansion:

- *Increase the number of users of the current data warehouse without adding data.* This alternative—which included conducting interviews, installing Business Objects on personal computers (PCs) and planning and conducting training classes—was projected to increase the number of regular users by more than 20.

- *Enhance the value of the data warehouse by adding data.* This alternative included adding data (e.g., month-to-date order activity; credit reason code; freight methods, terms, and charges; parts sales data; and service sales data) that would provide value to the users.

- *Expand the data warehouse by adding new subject areas.* Numerous new subject areas were identified and evaluated in terms of the impact to the customer and the effort to implement. One proposed new subject area was product tracking data, regulated by the FDA. ALARIS Medical must be able to track instruments by model, serial number, and specific location. (The FDA mandates this requirement in case of product recalls.) Having the information available in the warehouse would make this task easier.

■ *Improve data warehouse support.* This alternative included scheduling and conducting ongoing training classes, formalizing a portfolio of existing queries, identifying experts in each functional area, familiarizing more of the IS Department staff with the data warehouse tools, developing and implementing a marketing plan for the data warehouse, and dedicating a support team to the data warehouse.

The IS Department pursued all of these expansion opportunities while moving the warehouse on an evolutionary path that was guided by some top-level business decisions discussed in the next section.

Business Decisions and Systems Implications

Senior management had established a major corporate goal of growing sales significantly over the next several years, primarily through acquisitions. The company's former vice president and CFO had emphasized the importance of IT for a rapid growth and acquisition strategy. He also emphasized the importance of having a CEO who understands IT and its strategic value.

To prepare for acquisitions and rapid growth and to ensure Year 2000 (Y2K) systems compliance, senior management decided to invest $20 million in two key areas:

■ *Technology infrastructures*—Desktop systems were upgraded, and direct network connections were provided to replace dial-up. Expected benefits included company-wide access to information systems and increased security and control.

■ *Information systems*—Senior management decided to implement SAP as part of a two-year effort to upgrade the information systems. Expected benefits included improved operating efficiencies and control; customer electronic data interchange; resolution of Y2K issues; and a flexible, growth-oriented system.

The decision to implement SAP dictated decisions regarding systems compatibility. These decisions had a domino effect that necessitated three simultaneous systems conversions for the IS Department:

■ *Database—Oracle to Informix.* The SAP selection was based on Informix, so the Oracle database was converted to Informix.

■ *Query and reporting tool—Business Objects version 3.0 to Business Objects version 4.1.* The license on version 3.0 was expiring, and version 3.0 did not work with Informix. Users in the business units liked Business Objects, so version 3.0 was upgraded directly to version 4.1. This leapfrog-style upgrade (without going through intervening versions) required an additional effort from the IS Department.

■ *Desktop operating system—Windows 3.1 to Windows NT.* Business Objects version 4.1 did not work with Windows 3.1, so the Windows 3.1 operating systems on PCs were upgraded to Windows NT.

The Current Data Warehouse

The implementation of SAP in 1998 had a direct impact on the data warehouse. Management decided not to load historical data into the SAP system. The potential size of the database was one consideration. Data conversion was another.

The decision not to load historical data into SAP increased the importance of the warehouse as the only repository for retrospective data. SAP became a feeder system to add current data to the historical data in the data warehouse. In parallel with the SAP implementation, the warehouse had to be modified to accept feeder data from SAP.

The warehouse now resides on an Informix server. More data and new subject areas have been added, and more resources have been committed to support. The IS Department has developed a road show presentation to highlight the benefits of the warehouse. More than 10 different departments have seen the presentation. In addition, the IS Department developed a tiered training program. The first tier is "Beginner Business Objects" training. Recently, over 50 new users have been added.

Ongoing and Future Challenges

As it continues to evolve, the data warehouse presents numerous challenges in terms of training in the data structures, compatibility issues, and future directions.

Training in Data Structures

Several people highlighted the ongoing issues. Cathy Dooley, Contracts Administration Manager, talked about the data and training. Because she signs all contracts, she is acutely aware of the nuances of the customer and product data.

> The tool is easy, but the data is not! Knowledge of the data in there [the warehouse] is not widespread. There are too many nuances. We can't ask someone to run a report and be sure of the results. The issue is the complexity of the data. Product hierarchies can be difficult to understand.

> It's easy to get training on the tool—not on the data. The data warehouse is for expert users only. We need more training on the data. There have been some false alarms—fire alarms because of incorrect results coming from the data warehouse. People didn't understand the data.

Linda Noe, U.S. Service Manager, had similar concerns. She is the only warehouse user in her department because running reports requires an understanding of the service data. Because of difficulties in identifying and training new users, she developed some standardized queries for the sales force to use "as is."

Mariann Sievert, Manager of Sales Operations, also cautioned users:

> They need to be careful about how they set up queries. Business Objects always gives an answer, but they need to validate it—check one report against another. Sometimes we have to be creative with our deals, which can result in adjustments and delays in closing the books. That means there's a delay in getting the data into the warehouse, and they need to be aware of that.

Aware of the data and training challenges, the IS Department is wrestling with the issue of how to "certify" users at different levels—how to determine, for example, what it means to be classified as an "expert."

Compatibility Issues

Compatibility issues arise regularly. One compatibility issue relates to desktop workstations. The design engineers use Unix workstations, but the NT workstation—the business platform for the company—is required for warehouse access. According to Curt Baldwin, UNIX Administrator,

> The interactive stuff gets difficult with different platforms—for example, Word and the Unix workstations. We've got 800 NT workstations and 60 Unix workstations for engineers. Now all the engineers have two workstations—a Unix workstation and a PC with NT.

Another compatibility issue relates to external data and the outside sources of hospital data and group purchasing lists. The vendors selling this information—especially the ones that sell both data and the accompanying software packages—frequently change the format of the data to coincide with their software upgrades. The IS Department identified alternate sources of outside data in order to manage this risk.

Future Directions

The IS Department is evaluating SAP's information warehouses, which are integrated with the SAP software. If the IS Department determines that it makes good business sense, these miniwarehouses will be implemented. But there's still the question of whether to implement SAP's miniwarehouses in place of, or in concert with, the current warehouse. Alan Barnebey, Service Director, talked about some of the concerns:

> SAP is touted as an improvement over the Cullinet system. Some people think they won't need IT to program reports for them. Some said they won't need the data warehouse. Others said we should keep it anyway—there will be fewer people in IT available to give us systems reports. We may want to just keep the data warehouse.

Barnebey also talked about two other future challenges—mining the data in the warehouse and promoting do-it-yourself reporting by everyone in the organization, not just designated analysts.

> If we had enough time and people to do it, we'd be mining the data. The challenge is finding the time and people to do that. The engineers don't have the time—they spend their time doing design and change orders.

The design engineers preferred to have "chauffeurs" to produce special reports. Design engineers were not interested in learning the data and learning the query and reporting tools.

Uses and Benefits of the Data Warehouse

Business units throughout ALARIS Medical rely on the data warehouse to support daily operations. Mariann Sievert said it in a nutshell: "We might as well go home without it!" The specific uses and benefits of the warehouse vary by business unit, as discussed below.

Sales

Sales Operations uses the warehouse for several key functions that require both routine and ad hoc reporting: forecasting sales, evaluating trends, calculating commissions (e.g., exceptions), and supporting national accounts (e.g., responding to requests for proposal).

Kathleen Roth, Sales Analyst, was a member of the 1993 ET group that first investigated data warehousing technology. Using the warehouse several times per week to "run the numbers," she highlighted its importance in achieving sales objectives.

> Sales Operations figures out the sales objectives for the year for thermometers, pumps, disposables, etc. We determine objectives by looking at past sales, and we set objectives in categories: drug infusion instruments [pumps], drug infusion disposables, patient monitoring instruments, and patient monitoring disposables. Then every month we publish the rankings—a report card for the month and for the year-to-date.

She also emphasized the benefits of the warehouse for analyzing sales territories. She can evaluate virtual sales territories by moving hospitals to different sales representatives and running reports for simulated or virtual territories.

Steve Daluz, Sales Analyst, uses the warehouse daily. He talked about trend analysis.

> We do revenue/bed analyses. Pumps follow beds. There's a relationship between beds and pumps—not so much so for vital signs. Census is a better benchmark for vital signs. We look for patterns. If we "own" a facility, how many units should we have?

> When Finance closes the books, standard reports are available to Sales Operations—probe covers for thermometers, tubing for pumps, etc. I look in particular at the "A" accounts—for example, a $75,000 or more annual disposable account.

Trey Bullington, Business Analyst, talked about his work before and after the warehouse. He came from IMED (before the merger with IVAC, which then became ALARIS), where he did sales analysis.

> We had developed a very basic data warehouse for the sales department just prior to the merger. Before it was developed, the sales analysts used to do a lot of pencil and calculator work or data entry into spreadsheets. The warehouse was one of the pluses of the merger. It is well structured and has a broad base of support within the organization.

> I respond to requests from product managers and executives for ad hoc reports. Business Objects is too difficult for them to use. I can create requests for typical, repeat reports so they can do it themselves.

Service

ALARIS Medical provides a 10-year commitment for service on products—even after the last production build. (The oldest thermometers are 20 years old.) Marketing offers incentives on new products when an old product becomes obsolete. Obsolescence of a product is related to disposables. If the sales of related disposables are above a certain threshold, then the life of the product is extended.

Linda Noe uses the warehouse three to four times per week to analyze customer information, including servicing, repairs, and sales. She also evaluates business data for the Service Department, answering such questions as, How many service jobs were done last month? What are the trends? What is the productivity per technician?

The FDA regulates ALARIS Medical's products. Access to historical service data is mandatory. Since management decided not to load historical data into the new SAP system, the warehouse became the storehouse for historical service data as well as for handling many analyses of current SAP data. Analysts preferred to use one system, the warehouse, to analyze both historical and current data. Lee Phillips, Senior Systems Analyst, summarized the situation:

> For service tracking, we need legacy data. And we can't get that with SAP. In our business, we can't throw that data away. We've got to have access to it, and we want to get all the data from one source.

Linda Noe explained that "the FDA requires us to trend service data." The FDA also mandates a trace system so that the company knows the current location of all instruments. Since the Service Department sees the movement of equipment, Service is a convenient place to capture the data; and the warehouse has become the logical tool to research trace information.

Engineering

Linda Noe provides failure trending information to Engineering. This information is invaluable to the design engineers since early-life failures can provide warning signs related to design problems. As noted previously, however, the engineers prefer to receive these reports rather than to generate the reports themselves.

IS Department

A common theme across analysts in the business units at ALARIS Medical is "we don't want to be dependent on others to run queries. We want to do it ourselves." Thus, the IS Department has been able to reduce its workload by promoting self-sufficiency via the warehouse in training classes. Kathleen Roth told us that "four analysts and one manager in Sales Operations use the data warehouse. They learned through in-house classes."

Mary Thompson, Product Support Analyst, is one of numerous analysts at ALARIS Medical who like to be self-sufficient. She uses the warehouse several times per week, for reasons usually related to the renewal of a customer's contract.

> Eztrieve was not easy to use. Business Objects has made life simpler. I go in and create my own reports. I don't like to have to rely on other people. Some typical questions I answer myself are: How many repairs did the customer have? If there was no contract, how much would the repairs cost? What models have used a particular part number? What was the average response time for service calls during a specific period of time?

Contracts

Cathy Dooley, Manager of Contracts Administration, says that her contract-related information requests tend to be ad hoc.

> If we add a product to a government contract, we need to know "what's the lowest price we've sold it for?" If manufacturing wants to replace one product with another, we need to know "what's the impact?"

Key Success Factors

ALARIS Medical made an investment in data warehousing technology and successfully extracted business value from the investment. Some of the factors in that success are summarized below.

Satisfy Pressing Business Needs

The IS Department initiated the data warehouse because of pressing needs to satisfy an avalanche of reporting requests from the business units. The business units had pressing reporting requirements. Some requirements, such as trending service data, were mandated by the FDA.

Others, such as forecasting sales and calculating commissions, were mandated by the competitive business environment. The IS Department had limited resources, and the business units wanted to be self-sufficient. The data warehouse satisfied both.

Build a Model, Test It, and Let It Evolve

The ET group investigated data warehousing technologies and developed a preliminary design. After several iterations of the design, the IS Department built and populated a prototype data warehouse, which was tested during a "proof of concept" period. Then, instead of holding the warehouse back until the design was comprehensive, the IS Department rolled it out for the business units that wanted to use it. The design evolved as the business units articulated their needs. The structure and format of the data were changed four times.

Ensure Data Quality

The business units came to rely on the warehouse because they trusted the data. John Scholl emphasized the importance of establishing and proving data accuracy. He talked about investing the time required to reconcile data back to the general ledger and to trace errors back to the structure of the query.

Use Familiar Tools

John Scholl explained that "the users liked Business Objects, so we decided to continue using the same data warehouse with Business Objects." Because analysts in the business units liked Business Objects, the IS Department kept the query and reporting tool stable while the underlying warehouse evolved. For example, when the license on version 3.0 expired, version 3.0 was upgraded to version 4.1, even though the leapfrog-style upgrade required more work from the IS Department.

While this concept of using a familiar tool worked well for analysts in the business units, it has not worked as well for other potential users. The design engineers, for example, may not find Business Objects easy to use. To facilitate their hands-on use of the data warehouse, something more user-friendly (e.g., semi-canned reports available on the intranet) may need to be considered.

Provide Training and Support

Mariann Sievert summarized why the data warehouse had become so popular at ALARIS Medical: "It's easy to learn how to use; it's well supported by the organization, and there's always a need for more and better information."

People Interviewed

Curt Baldwin, UNIX Administrator

Alan Barnebey, Director, Service

Rick Bernstein, Principal Database Administrator

Trey Bullington, Business Analyst

Barbara Burkett, Director, Corporate Communications

Steve Daluz, Sales Analyst

Cathy Dooley, Manager, Contracts Administration

Thomas P. Murray, Senior Manager, SAP Project

Linda Noe, U.S. Service Manager

Lee A. Phillips, CPIM, Senior Systems Analyst

Lori Robinson, Sales Analyst

Kathleen Roth, Sales Analyst

John G. Scholl, Manager, Business Support Systems

Mariann Sievert, Manager, Sales Operations

Mary Thompson, Product Support Analyst

Paul C. Trivino, Principal Information Engineer

Endnotes

1. Company profile information is from the ALARIS Medical Systems' Web site at www.alarismed.com.

2. ALARIS, ALARIS Medical Systems, IVAC, and IMED are trademarks or registered trademarks of ALARIS Medical Systems, Inc.

Kraft Foods, Inc.

Case Summary

When Kraft Foods, Inc., first adopted data warehousing, the company was attempting to integrate a large number of disparate business units under a "one company" philosophy. The goal was to operate as a single entity with respect to its customers. Standing in the way of realizing this goal was Kraft's unwieldy legacy systems environment. Different product divisions had developed their own systems to perform similar tasks. As a result, the whole of the company's information about, say, a customer could be distributed across dozens of incompatible systems. Consolidating these systems made sense, but it takes time, and Kraft had urgent information needs. To make the situation even more challenging, Kraft was dealing with huge volumes of data—for example, the line items on every invoice it generates. Data warehousing was an obvious part of its total systems solution. This case provides an overview of the company and its technology environment, then focuses in depth on three different data warehousing initiatives, summarized in table 5.1.

Company Profile

Kraft Foods, Inc., is a subsidiary of Philip Morris Companies, Inc. Headquartered in Northfield, Illinois, Kraft Foods is the largest manufacturer and marketer of retail packaged food in the United States, with 1998 operating revenues of $17.2 billion.

Kraft Foods has grown through a series of acquisitions. In 1985, General Foods bought Oscar Mayer Foods but did not integrate its operations. In 1985, Philip Morris bought General Foods. Philip Morris then acquired Kraft, Inc., in 1988 and merged it with General Foods in

Table 5.1
Summary of the Kraft Foods, Inc.,
Data Warehousing Initiatives Examined in This Case

Warehouse Name	Business Situation	Technology Used
Shared Services/ Time and Expense Reporting Data Mart	A new central organizational unit was formed to handle accounting and HR administrative services for all divisions, which had previously handled their own services with their own systems. The new unit did not have an integrated decision support environment. Therefore, data requests from the divisions required time-consuming and expensive manual sorting and summarizing of paper records.	Current ■ A new travel and expense transaction processing system (Travel Master). ■ Red Brick for data storage. ■ Microsoft Access database for data queries. Planned enhancements ■ Replace Access with Business Objects for queries. ■ Make expense report transmittal and warehouse queries available via the Internet.
Sales/Operations Decision Support/The Category Profit and Loss Data Mart	The corporate decision to eliminate the VM mainframe operating system required replacement of a mainframe based reporting tool (System W) that was heavily used by divisional personnel to analyze sales and operations data. Replacing System W required reprogramming the many hundreds of standard reports in use. However, errors, poor development practices, and redundancy in the reports made it desirable to enhance the model environment and optimize the business processes before reprogramming the reports. This, in turn, required a cross-functional team approach guided by division systems personnel.	■ Essbase for data storage, access, and reporting.

Table 5.1
Summary of the Kraft Foods, Inc.,
Data Warehousing Initiatives Examined in This Case   *(Continued)*

Warehouse Name	Business Situation	Technology Used
Advertising/Promotion Systems Data Mart	Divisions organize and manage consumer advertising and trade promotions for their products. Historically, each division had its own systems for tracking advertising and promotions. KAPS—a new transaction processing system—replaced these many operational systems in 1998. A data warehouse was needed to enable reporting from KAPS. Concurrently, the corporate decision to eliminate the VM mainframe operating system made it necessary to replace the PICS reporting system—a system heavily used by many divisions for analyzing 12 years of historical data (which must remain separate from KAPS data).	See figure 5.3 for schematic. ▪ Data from KAPS and a variety of mainframe advertising and financial systems are extracted using COBOL extracts and stored in a Red Brick data warehouse. ▪ Historical sales data are stored in a DB2 database. ▪ Historical promotion data are stored in Essbase. ▪ Promotion data stored in Essbase can be accessed by Excel or Business Objects. ▪ Business Objects must be used to access data from Red Brick data warehouse or DB2 database.

1989, creating Kraft General Foods. For some time, Kraft and General Foods continued to operate somewhat autonomously, each maintaining its own headquarters. In 1995, they reorganized into a single operating company, Kraft Foods, Inc.

The new organization structure of Kraft Foods (see figure 5.1) has a common sales force to present one face to the customer, a common operations unit to optimize production and logistics across the brand groups, and a shared finance and systems group. In addition, it has a number of marketing groups, responsible for developing financial targets and promotion plans for the major brand groups. The new structure has proven very successful in achieving the returns sought by Philip

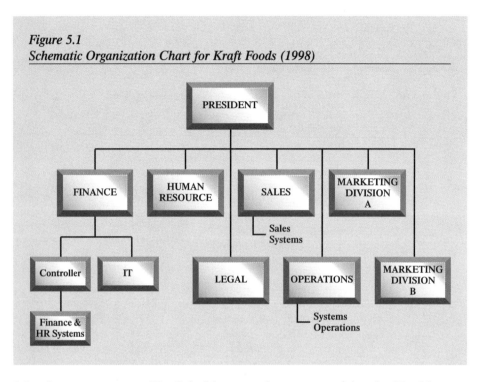

Figure 5.1
Schematic Organization Chart for Kraft Foods (1998)

Morris management. Kraft holds a number one position in 17 of its top 20 product categories.

IT and Kraft

The IT function at Kraft Foods is distributed. That is, issues related to IT infrastructure (e.g., corporate networking, hardware acquisition and operation, and desktop computing standards) are handled on a centralized basis for the whole organization. Issues related to IS applications (i.e., the uses of information technology) are distributed to various organizational units. This structural arrangement is designed to achieve the benefits of centralized IT purchases and support operating costs while ensuring that internal customer groups have systems that meet their specialized needs. If this structure has a drawback, it is that the infrastructure group and the applications groups are connected via a dotted line relationship, and some coordination difficulties can be expected to result.

At Kraft, the unit responsible for the IT infrastructure is called "IT." It is headed by Steve Finnerty, Kraft's Chief Technical Officer, who reports to Jim Kinney, Senior Vice President, Information Systems. Kinney reports to James P. Dollive, Senior Vice President, Finance and Information Systems. The units responsible for IS applications are called "Information Systems groups," and there is one each for Finance and HR, Sales and Customer Service, and Operations. The Finance and HR systems group, headed by John Helmerci, reports to the Controller, Jack F. Mowrer (who in turn reports to Dollive). This group is responsible for the IS applications needs of the corporate headquarters units (finance and HR) and for the financial systems of the marketing divisions. Similarly, the Sales and Customer Service systems unit and the Operations systems unit report to the heads of those divisions (See figure 5.1).

Our focus in this case is on the use of data warehousing within the Finance and HR Systems area (but excluding the HR area). Therefore, within the headquarters systems area, we looked at data warehousing as it applies to the common financial systems (e.g., general ledger, accounts payable). Within the divisional systems area, we looked at data warehousing in relation to the advertising and promotions systems and to the divisions' decision support needs with respect to sales and operational data and administrative data. (See figure 5.2.)

As expected in an organization that grew through acquisition, by 1995 Kraft Foods had accumulated a diverse portfolio of unintegrated transaction processing applications. In 1994, for instance, the company had 22 separate general-ledger systems and 18 different purchasing systems. (Today, it has consolidated all retail general ledgers and accounts payable systems.) Because information about customers, products, and other entities was dispersed across a number of different systems, managers at Kraft had a hard time answering even simple questions about the business. Irv Coleman and Ken Nelson, Business Systems Managers in the Finance and HR systems group, explained:

> After the mergers, we had three salespeople calling on the same store. But you can't go in with one face to the customer unless you have one system. The customer wants discounts based on their total tonnage of all Kraft foods. With our old systems, there was no way that we could tell them that total.

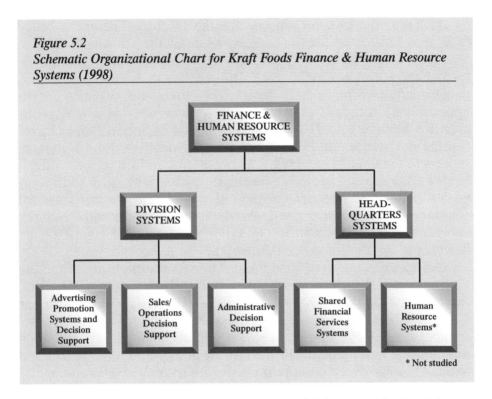

Figure 5.2
Schematic Organizational Chart for Kraft Foods Finance & Human Resource Systems (1998)

In 1994, Kraft began a common systems initiative with the ultimate objective of enabling integrated decision support—the ability to analyze data at various levels of summarization across divisions and to answer specific questions about status and trends. To gain decision support capability, systems specialists at Kraft embarked on a two-pronged strategy involving transaction system consolidation and data warehousing.

System consolidation can mean two things. First, it can mean replacing many systems used for the same purpose (e.g., general-ledger systems) with a smaller number (ideally one) of common systems, so called because they are used in common across a number of business units. In addition to enabling decision support, common systems promote effective use of a company's human resources. Irv Coleman explained: "You can't move people easily from one division to another without common systems. The learning costs are too high otherwise."

Second, system consolidation can mean integrating or linking different kinds of systems (e.g., sales and financial applications) at the level of detailed transaction data rather than at the summary level. (When systems are linked at the summary level, we refer to them as "interfaced," not "integrated.") Generally speaking, integrated systems provide greater scope for decision support than interfaced systems, but systems integration is a very difficult task. Kraft Foods has been more successful in achieving system commonality than systems integration. The first area to consolidate data at the enterprise level was Sales. According to George Haettinger and Dennis Pankow of Kraft's IT unit:

> The systems used in Sales were built over the years based on diverse business cultures and practice. They provided needed information but were not integrated with all the business processes at Kraft that required access to sales information. To consolidate these systems, Sales spent several years cleaning and aligning data to make it accessible for field sales personnel.

The movement toward a "one company" Kraft Foods "gave us the green light to consolidate our [financial information] systems," said John Helmerci, Director of Finance and HR Systems. But achieving common systems proved to be "more than a little challenge. These [business] processes are core issues for people in the divisions; they live by what has proven effective and has been built over a period of years."

Common systems meant gaining consensus across a number of divisions and functions about ways of doing business. For example, key business terms like "customer" meant different things in different divisions. Therefore, consolidating systems meant standardizing business terminology. Also, big differences in business practices across the divisions proved to be major obstacles to the consolidation effort. Today, however, "every variable means the same thing across all divisions," Helmerci says.

He added that there are two ways to achieve systems commonality. The first is "slash and burn." This approach defines the new process and moves everyone to it without compromise. It would not work at Kraft because of the great complexity in the business practices of different entities, and "you need the knowledge of the people" to build good systems. The second way, which Helmerci took, was a more classical reengineering approach. Large cross-functional teams were formed to work toward consensus on the best business practice. This approach takes longer, because "often what the people think is important really isn't [from a systems point of view]. But our view is that we don't go ahead until we get agreement." This paced, yet effective, process ensured that the new common systems were successfully adopted and used.

Since 1994, Kraft Foods has installed a common general-ledger system, a common travel and expense (T&E) reporting system, a common accounts payable system, a common payroll system, and a common capital payment and fixed assets system. Also under way at the time of our data collection were projects for a common promotion and accounting system (called KAPS) and a common decision support system (involving data warehousing).

Despite considerable progress, complete systems integration is not the current direction at Kraft. The major applications groups, such as Financial Systems and Advertising/Promotion Systems, are still separate. Summary data are shared across applications via interfaces, but it is not easy to link individual sales transactions, for example, to their direct financial impacts. (By contrast, fully integrated enterprise systems like SAP, built around a common database, link sales and financial data for each individual transaction.) Systems specialists at Kraft believe that full systems integration is not possible today for financial and organizational reasons. Irv Coleman said, "The cost of something like SAP would be astronomical for us, and it would take several years to implement."

History of Data Warehousing

When systems specialists at Kraft first began to think about how to handle decision support needs (information access and reporting) in the "one company" environment, they explored the possibility of an enterprise data warehousing solution. Such a solution would address all functional areas and applications groups within the organization. The first step would be to create common definitions for all data elements used in the company. John Helmerci said:

The enterprise approach might have been possible for us if we were starting with common systems, common data definitions, and common business processes. But we had legacy systems, each with its own database, database management system, and data definitions.

For a company like this, an enterprise-wide approach is an incomprehensible task. No one could even agree on the meaning of a "customer." We talked about trying to sell an enterprise data warehouse to the organization, how much it would cost, who would fund it. It would have been expensive just for the environment [the hardware and software needed for the data warehouse], and then you would have needed a massive team effort to determine requirements and data definitions. We decided against it. Sales would be interested in seeing common data definitions throughout the company, but getting other groups to buy in to the definitions would take too much time. We'd never get the buy-in. They'd never see the benefit. So we decided to break it into pieces.

Applications of Data Warehousing Technology

Kraft adopted the strategy of developing small, discrete data warehouses (often called data marts) to handle the inquiry and reporting needs associated with a particular applications systems, such as T&E reporting or category profit and loss analysis. This approach capitalized on the synergies that had been created during the consolidation of the operational transaction processing systems. During that process, people from different units in the company had agreed on a definition for each of the relevant business terms and had standardized some business practices. Consequently, setting up data warehouses to handle reporting needs and inquiries such as "what is the status of Jones' April 11 expense report?" was a relatively straightforward exercise.

Why didn't Kraft use the transaction processing systems themselves to handle inquiries and reporting needs? Doing so would have severely reduced the operating performance of those transaction systems. For example, if someone tried to run a complex report against the operational T&E system, the system would slow down, and the productivity of people entering T&E data would have been affected. John Helmerci explained:

> For us [at Kraft], data warehousing is largely an operational solution. We collect unbelievable amounts of information on events, such as coupons, in our transaction processing systems. Later, we try to find out, for example, whether we got product sales lift due to

a particular promotion campaign. To try to analyze this data with our existing technology would slow down our transaction processing systems, so we warehouse the data and then query it.

By decoupling the data warehouse for inquiry and reporting needs from the underlying transaction system for collecting and computing data about basic business events, Kraft maintains good system performance (i.e., response times) both for the people making queries and for those handling business events.

After Kraft abandoned the idea of an enterprise-wide data warehousing solution, the first group to implement a data warehouse was Sales. The sales history data warehouse was implemented using the Red Brick multidimensional OLAP (on-line analytical processing) product. It was organized by the business-relevant dimensions of period, customer, product, and adjustments. Data from the sales transaction systems were loaded into the warehouse weekly, using custom COBOL programs to extract data from the DB2 sales system database. Today, this warehouse has 2,500 users who perform 63,000 queries per week with an access tool that was custom developed using PowerBuilder.

John Helmerci's group was not far behind Sales. To date, the Finance and HR systems group has implemented data warehouses for T&E reporting, advertising and promotion, and category profit and loss queries and reporting. Future plans include warehouses for marketing and HR. Each of these data warehousing initiatives is discussed separately later in this report.

Data Warehousing Technology Standards
By the end of 1995, the IT unit had become aware that the systems units for Sales and Finance and HR were proposing a number of different projects that fell under the heading of data warehousing. This prompted the IT unit to research the basic tools and technologies of data warehousing and to define corporate-wide technology standards. The purpose of technology standards is to help companies achieve cost savings from volume license purchases, reduced maintenance expenses, and lower learning costs.

We spoke with George Haettinger, Business Systems Manager, and Dennis Pankow, Associate Business Systems Manager, both from the

IT unit. Both were somewhat skeptical about the faddishness of data warehousing terminology. "We've been doing it since 1976, but we called it 'decision support systems.'"

One of the chief objectives of the IT unit was to separate current transaction data from the historical data used for warehousing and queries. In 1996, the IT unit published an internal white paper on the technical architecture of data warehousing.

> Historical data and current data have different properties. We need a "system of record" and we need to warehouse data that is historical. You don't update historical data though you can restate [aggregate, categorize, etc.] it. One important factor in storing historical information is to dimensionalize data properly in the transaction systems. When data is properly categorized, it is then possible to perform restatement for changes in the business.

The data warehousing framework of the IT unit specified standard technologies for each of three different functions: data capture, data storage, and data access/reporting. The standards were selected to address the overall needs of Kraft Foods. And for most of the data warehousing initiatives of the Finance and HR Systems groups at Kraft, these standards were very functional. For example, the IS groups used products from Red Brick Systems for storing data in the warehouse. For access and reporting, they adopted Business Objects. But in the data capture area (extracting data from core transaction processing systems), the IS groups found that it was more practical to use customized COBOL programs rather than the standard tool. (See table 5.2 for notes on some of the technologies discussed in this case.)

The Uses of Data Warehousing at Kraft Foods

This section describes three data warehousing initiatives of the Finance and HR Systems group at Kraft: a data warehouse for shared services T&E reporting, a data warehouse for category profit and loss data in the sales/operations decision support area, and a data warehouse for advertising/promotion data.

Table 5.2
Notes on Technologies Used in the Kraft Foods, Inc., Data Marts[1]

Technology	Use at Kraft Foods	Comments
Red Brick Systems	■ The IT Unit's standard for warehouse data storage and online analytical processing (OLAP). ■ Used in the Time and Expense Reporting Data Mart. ■ Used (for KAPS and other data) in conjunction with Essbase in the Advertising/Promotion Systems Data Mart.	Red Brick Systems' core product is a two-dimensional relational data warehouse engine. Recently the company began offering an OLAP product. Before that, customers used other products for OLAP (e.g., Business Objects) or wrote their own tools for data access (as with the current version of the Time and Expense Reporting Data Mart). Red Brick's product has excellent performance in query handling for large warehouses. It does not, however, easily accommodate data changes by the end user (which are frequently required during planning and budgeting as in the Category Profit and Loss Data Mart, for example).
Essbase	■ Used (for historical advertising data) in conjunction with Red Brick in the Advertising/Promotion Systems Data Mart. ■ Used in lieu of the Red Brick/Business Objects IT Unit standard in the Category Profit and Loss Data Mart.	Essbase uses a proprietary multidimensional data structure (called data cubes) in contrast to Red Brick Systems' two-dimensional relational structure. Essbase has excellent performance with smaller warehouses with a few static dimensions, as is the case in financial consolidation and reporting. In addition, Essbase supports end-user data changes as needed in the Category Profit and Loss Data Mart.
Business Objects	■ The IT Unit's standard for data access and reporting. ■ Planned use in the Time and Expense Reporting Data Mart. ■ Used in conjunction with Excel in the Advertising/Promotion Systems Data Mart.	This product began as an executive information system (EIS) tool. It was modified and remarketed as an OLAP tool. It uses the traditional EIS approach of loading data onto the desktop computer for query/analysis. It accommodates data from both Essbase and Red Brick (as needed in the Advertising/Promotion Systems Data Mart), consolidating the data on the desktop, not in the data warehouse.

[1] Dave Petrie, doctoral candidate at the Program in Information Science, Claremont Graduate University, provided helpful input to this table.

Shared Services T&E Reporting and
Accounts Payable Data Marts

In 1994, as part of the "one company" initiative, Kraft Foods established a shared services unit in San Antonio, Texas, to provide accounts payable, T&E, payroll, and HR services on a centralized basis to all Kraft divisions. Before this reorganization, each division handled its own administrative services with its own systems.

Almost immediately, division controllers inundated the shared services unit with requests for information, analysis, and reports. For example, as a cost-cutting measure, Kraft management determined that travel costs between headquarters locations should be reduced. Controllers wanted to know how many people were traveling the New York-Chicago route. To answer this question, shared services staff had to pull paper T&E reports from files and analyze them by hand—a process that took 20 people two days to complete. This request was only one of many. Management wanted to know who was doing the most traveling and how their departments were doing on T&E spending, among many other questions.

The Finance systems unit began addressing these needs simultaneously with a two-pronged approach. On the one hand, they implemented a new common T&E transaction system with improved functionality. On the other, they built decision support capability using data warehousing technology.

The T&E system employs the client server architecture. The heart of the system is a mainframe-based package called Travel Master. Individual travelers (and their administrative assistants) provide input to the system via a Visual Basic front end (interactive form) on their PCs. (The front-end application transmits the data to the mainframe system via e-mail.) When they submit information about a trip, the system returns a trip number that travelers put on their envelopes of receipts, which are then sent to San Antonio through interoffice mail.

When the Finance and HR systems group began building the T&E data warehouse, the corporate IT unit had not yet selected a standard tool for data access and reporting. The controllers' information needs were so pressing that a team headed by Brian Onufer, Business Systems Manager, found a solution that met their needs before the standard was chosen. In his expedient solution, data are extracted from the mainframe transaction system and stored in a Red Brick data warehouse, which is then accessed by a Microsoft Access database. When faced with a request for information, financial specialists in San Antonio select the most appropriate Access query from a predefined list and set the appropriate parameters (e.g., date range, geography). The next steps planned for this warehouse include replacing the Access database queries with the corporate standard tool (Business Objects) and rolling out this tool to financial specialists in the divisions.

One of the lessons from this project was that determining people's information analysis and reporting needs is an iterative process. During the project, the design team worked with users to identify the most important types of information requests. But now, as people have more experience working with the data warehouse, the systems specialists are getting more input about how people want to use the decision support system.

A similar data warehousing initiative is currently under way in the shared services group around accounts payable processing and decision support. Kraft, like many large companies, wants to improve cash flow management and provide a consolidated view for answering accounts payable customer service questions. To address this business need, the Finance systems group developed an interim solution using a Microsoft SQL server. The Red Brick data warehouse is fed by the check-writing system, the workflow system, and banking reports of checks cleared. The completed warehouse will give corporate finance specialists a complete picture of cash flows and answer such questions as Who is our top vendor of X? and How long does it take us to complete the payment cycle for Y? Also, the warehouse will provide one-stop shopping for answering accounts payable customer service questions. Kraft is also looking at leveraging the data warehouse to provide employee self-service for accounts payable status via the intranet. The long-term vision is to be able to look at general-ledger expenses in the data warehouse and to drill down into accounts payable data.

Brian Onufer's experience in the T&E and accounts payables warehousing projects has led him to conclude that data warehousing is a viable alternative to systems integration for organizations like Kraft Foods, as long as data elements are consistently defined across the systems. He notes that data warehousing is easier when the feeder systems have already been consolidated into a relational database; otherwise developers must spend lots of time working with users to create and balance the data across the systems.

Sales/Operations Decision Support/
The Category Profit and Loss Data Mart

The development of the data mart for the sales and operations decision support area was prompted by the need to replace an old mainframe decision support tool. As part of Kraft Food's technology simplification project, the decision was made to replace the VM mainframe operating system. This decision, in turn, meant that a replacement had to be found for all applications that ran on VM. One of them was a decision support tool called System W, which had been used in Kraft Foods since 1983. At that time, System W was considered to be the best financial analysis tool available. All three pre-merged companies—General Foods, Kraft, and Oscar Mayer—had independently acquired it. With the company's stated direction of eliminating the VM System, Kraft was forced to replace System W.

By some accounts, the replacement of System W was long overdue. It was not user friendly. According to Irv Coleman, "You had to be a programmer to use it." (Nevertheless, analysts and many senior managers in the divisions used it, because it filled an urgent need.) In addition, it was a single-user tool, which meant that only one person could use it at a time. The replacement—a multidimensional OLAP tool—eliminates the single-user constraint.

A selection team of System W users, steering committee members, and IS specialists was formed. Several products were considered, including Hyperion, TM1, and Essbase. During the selection process, each vendor was brought in and given a simple business situation and the same dataset. Among the evaluation criteria was how fast the user could build a decision model and run it against the data. In February 1997, Essbase was selected for pilot testing by three user groups (two divisions and one headquarters unit). The proof of concept was intended to see how well the new tool could mimic the functionality currently available without forcing users to adopt common data structures and naming conventions. At that point, the plan was to reengineer the old System W models for greater analytic power and commonality.

By the end of August, the pilot users were convinced that Essbase provided great benefits with less work. In fact, they were so convinced that the CFO decided to roll forward the timeframe for replacing System W. The end of 1998 was set as the new deadline for eliminating the use of System W for analyzing data from the entire suite of transaction systems used by the divisions (including sales and operational systems, not just financial). The project to replace System W was given the acronym SWEET (for System W Elimination Essbase Transformation).

From the perspective of Irv Coleman's system support group, the decision to advance the System W replacement schedule had several drawbacks. First, the intended user community had grown.

> We had been anticipating 125 users, and we negotiated our site license agreement on that basis. Now we have 335 users and we still have not completed the conversion. We're already going back [to the Steering Committee] to ask for more money. We may soon have as many as 600 users across the company. I'm afraid we're going too fast.

Second, Coleman was concerned that there would not be time to reengineer all the System W models before the changeover to Essbase. The population of known System W models in Kraft is approximately 2,600. Of these, 900 were eliminated altogether, and 700 were identified as duplicated. This left 1,000 models to be transformed.

Transformation could be done in one of two ways. The first was to convert the 1,000 System W models into Essbase models one for one, retaining the existing business processes and technology support for combining data from various base applications. Under this approach, it was expected that the conversion could be accomplished in six weeks by a team of two people (one financial analyst and one systems person) per application area (of which there were 13).

The second approach was to convert the 1,000 System W models into an estimated 350 Essbase models while incorporating some best practices and adopting a "one company" concept. This approach was expected to require a six-person cross-functional team (four financial analysts and two systems specialists) for each of the 13 applications areas.

Although the second approach was more expensive and time-consuming, it had important long-term benefits. It would significantly reduce the complexity of the information processing environment at Kraft Foods, leading to much lower operating costs. It would also make things easier when the base transaction systems were upgraded. Finally, it would improve the information flows across the company from functions to divisions to corporate, supporting the "one company" concept.

Why was it necessary to do so much elimination and reprogramming of the System W models? Many of the existing System W models had been developed by financial analysts, not by systems staff. There was duplication of effort and lack of shared knowledge about what models were available. Also, standard Information Systems development practices were not followed in all cases.

Aware that the replacement of System W provided an opportunity for changing these business practices, the Steering Committee established a new policy about Essbase model development. Henceforth, the systems unit would develop all models, and the analysts would run them. Ultimately, having a centralized model development team will make it much easier to ensure the use of standards about acceptable data sources and common approaches to calculating certain variables. This, in turn, will increase the likelihood that different analysts would get the same answers to the same query, thus reducing the potential for conflict in decision-making sessions.

The Profit and Loss data mart would be populated with new data from the transaction processing source systems once a month. Once a quarter, the data mart would be revised to include summary results for the latest quarter.

Because Essbase is designed as an extension of the Excel spreadsheet program, with which most financial analysts are very familiar, end-user training was not expected to be much of a problem. During the pilot conversion exercise that preceded SWEET, one day of training from a third-party provider proved sufficient. For the rollout, a train-the-trainer approach would be used. The biggest part of the end-user training would be to explain the structure of the data in the data mart and the organization and naming of the models.

Essbase training for the IS developers was more involved, and demand for people with Essbase development skills is great. Kraft has found it difficult to fill positions with experienced people and has lost some trained specialists to software vendors. Ultimately, Kraft believes that the best strategy is to build internal expertise, despite potential difficulties in retaining in-house experts. But Kraft has used external vendors to meet tight deadlines.

Advertising/Promotion Systems Data Mart

The end customers of Kraft Foods' products are individual consumers and households. Kraft Foods tries to influence the consumer's choice by advertising, which is generally done by the marketing divisions for individual brands, such as coffee, cereal, and cheese. (Some advertising is coordinated at the corporate level for major events such as the Super Bowl. For these activities, each division participates by contributing part of its advertising budget to the overall cost of the event.) The process of allocating marketing units' resources to end-consumer advertising is referred to within Kraft as "consumer." But Kraft does not sell directly to the end customer; it sells to grocery stores and other food retailers. To influence demand at the store level, Kraft's sales force plans promotions that are referred to as "trade."

There is a big difference between consumer and trade. First, sales revenues are measured against trade deals, not against consumer deals. Second, different groups within Kraft are responsible for the two types of deals—marketing units for consumer advertising and sales units and finance for trade promotions. Information about consumer and trade activity at Kraft has always been processed in separate systems. Development of the new client-server transaction system was a joint effort of Finance/Division systems and Sales. KAPS (Kraft Advertising and Promotion System), which went live in August 1998, replaces a host of old General Foods legacy systems used in the divisions and processes the consumer portion of the business.

KAPS was estimated to have a reasonable return from eliminating the costs of operating and supporting multiple systems. The new system also promotes the "one company" vision and creates an infrastructure to support future business and systems enhancements.

Part of the KAPS development project was the KAPS data warehouse, designed to handle queries and reporting against the new transaction processing system. The architecture for this data warehouse followed the IT standards: COBOL was used as the data extraction tool, Red Brick was used for data storage, and Business Objects was selected for data access and reporting needs.

The decision to retire VM at the end of 1998 forced the Finance and HR systems group to replace the PICS system. PICS, another General Foods legacy system, is a mission-critical, mainframe-based decision support system used by the brand divisions. Containing 12 years of historical data, PICS was fed by 13 different source systems, with data about advertising, finance, and sales.

Replacing PICS was no easy task, according to Ken Nelson, who oversaw both the KAPS project and the PICS replacement. Over the 12 years of history contained in PICS, division structures and products had changed. And before the consolidation of sales and financial systems, the feeder systems to PICS didn't even have a common product numbering system. (The new data warehouse that replaces PICS will be driven by the product master field fed from the sales system.) Perhaps most difficult of all were the cultural issues. Nelson said:

> PICS is very ingrained in the East. When John [Helmerci] first mentioned in a meeting that we were planning to phase out PICS, the users were very concerned. They called a meeting with me scheduled for three weeks later, and at that meeting they presented the critical nature of PICS and its importance to business. They made it clear that any replacement must be equally good.

Further complicating the replacement of PICS were the cultural differences between the old Kraft and the old General Foods. "The East [eastern divisions, former General Foods] wouldn't take what the West [former Kraft] wanted, and vice versa." Nelson took on the task of designing the PICS replacement because of his role in KAPS. But he noted that, longer term, the ownership of both KAPS (a joint finance/sales system) and the replacement for PICS (with more than 50 percent of its data coming from sales systems) was an open question. He continued:

> I couldn't dictate the best data warehousing solution to the data owners [of PICS]. That would have speeded development up, but it wasn't the right thing to do. The data owners [the divisions] have to own their data warehouse. Otherwise, they won't use it. I owned KAPS, so I could lead the KAPS data warehouse solution, but that was not true for PICS. The downside of shared ownership is that it's hard to convince people.

During discussions around the development of the KAPS data warehouse, the East and West divisions lobbied for very different solutions. "The old General Foods divisions came up with a solution that ran everything through PICS. This would have added more complexity, instead of reducing it. This made it easier to move to the new data warehouse." But the architecture of that warehouse is not as simple as originally envisioned, because of the PICS users' need for 12 years of historical sales and promotion data.

Transaction systems like KAPS generally contain only a few days, weeks, or months of current data (depending on the business). Historical data are archived (warehoused) for subsequent retrieval, analysis, and reporting. When a new system like KAPS comes on line, it starts with only the bare minimum of historical data in its databases. All data subsequently archived from KAPS are stored under the Red Brick system. But that solution was not possible for the historical data from the old sales system (stored in DB2) and from the old promotion systems (stored in Essbase). (The different data storage schemes were required by differences in data models—ways in which items of information are represented to the computer and to human users for purposes of storage and retrieval. It would be prohibitively expensive, and likely error prone, to try to remodel historical data for storage under a different scheme.) Therefore, the KAPS/PICS replacement data warehouse now has three different storage approaches rather than one.

A further wrinkle is that Essbase supports access and reporting via Excel, while Red Brick and DB2 do not. Since many users prefer Excel over Business Objects as an access tool (because they already know Excel), the KAPS/PICS replacement data warehouse will give users the option of accessing historical promotion data via either Excel or Business Objects. (However, those who wish to access KAPS data and historical sales data will have to use Business Objects.) See figure 5.3 for a diagram of the architecture of the KAPS/PICS replacement data warehouse.

Why, then, didn't the KAPS data warehouse team just bow to the PICS users' preference for Excel? First, Business Objects was the standard set by the IT unit. But, more important, said Ken Nelson,

> Excel versus Business Objects interface is night and day. Business Objects is a query tool. Excel is a spreadsheet. You can't use Excel

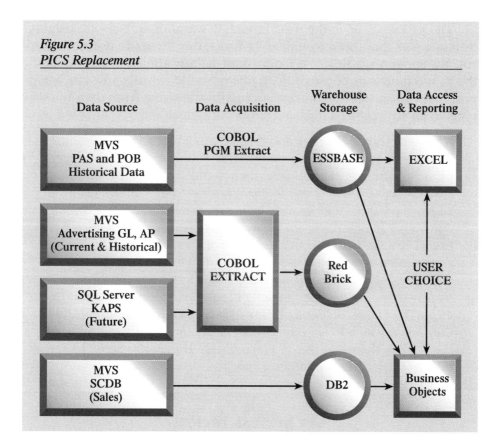

Figure 5.3
PICS Replacement

against the Red Brick data storage scheme. Business Objects lets the answer to a query be sent to you through the Internet. And there are ways around the ease of use issue. We are trying to develop a set of standard queries, so the users won't always have to design their own.

But again, the situation is not simple. If there are too many canned reports, maintaining the reports will become a headache for the systems unit. And Business Objects has a complex licensing scheme with three different pricing levels (for users who read only standard reports, users who do simple queries, and users who do advanced queries). An alternative solution that provides access to data and reports via the Kraft intranet might reduce costs and address the issue of ease of use.

The proof will be in the use of the data warehouse. Nelson's original estimate was that there would be 41 users, but there are not that many yet. We spoke with Business Consultant Rita Fridman, who worked on the KAPS data warehouse project. She described vividly how much support many users need to make a successful transition from their old systems to an entirely new decision support regime:

> After we cleaned the data and created models based on user interviews, we had to persuade people that the new models produced valid answers. We ran the new reports and showed them that they gave the same answers as the old reports—to the penny. Then we had to show them that we were giving them a better tool for drilling down and summarizing up. They didn't like Business Objects at first: They thought it wasn't user friendly. I told them, "We'll give you training and an easy user guide." I developed the guide; it was only four pages long. But even so, I had to take them through it step by step. You have to remember that these people are not technical. They know accounting. But they only know one system. And they don't want a PC in their office. Every time I do something for them, I ask them, "Is this too technical?" If they say "yes," I keep making it simpler until they say "no."

Key Success Factors

Benefits from Data Warehousing in Addition to Data Mining

Data warehousing can provide significant financial and business benefits to a company, even if the warehoused data are not used to support data mining. The nonmining benefits come from improved systems consolidation and integration and better management reporting.

Data warehousing can enable an organization to make progress toward systems consolidation and integration. Often, however, complete integration requires major changes in the design of the source transaction processing systems.

Data warehousing can provide significant benefits even if complete systems integration is not achieved. Structurally complex companies can benefit from stand-alone data marts, even if these marts are not completely subsumed under a common data warehousing architecture and an enterprise data model.

Manage Human and Organizational Change

Systems consolidation and integration *are* organizational change. Resistance can be expected. Therefore, careful change management is essential to the success of data warehousing used as a tool for systems integration.

The most time-consuming part of a data warehousing initiative involves arriving at consensus about data names and definitions and cleaning historical data. The process of readying the data for a data warehousing initiative provides a wonderful opportunity for effective change management.

Users can be very reluctant to accept new query and reporting tools, even when the new tools are demonstrably better than the old ones. Users must be absolutely convinced about the quality of the data accessible via the new tools, and even then, they may require much hand-holding.

Build in Flexibility

Determining people's requirements for information analysis and reporting is an iterative process. People often cannot fully articulate their needs and how they will use data and analysis/reporting tools until they have worked with them. Therefore, the design of the warehouse has to be sufficiently flexible to permit changes.

There is tension between the need for standards to reduce the cost of system maintenance and the need to find the right data warehousing tool for a particular application. Many factors must be considered in selecting the appropriate tools.

Organizations can often benefit from quick-and-dirty data warehousing implementations that take shortcuts in data modeling and architecture. Note, however, that this approach may require subsequent downstream costs to improve the performance, data quality, and maintainability of the warehouse.

Manage Technical Personnel

Data warehousing does not fit neatly into the categories traditionally used to manage IT—applications and infrastructure. It can legitimately be said to belong to both. Therefore, it is likely that some conflict over data warehousing will develop between IT infrastructure groups and IT applications development and maintenance groups.

With a rapidly evolving technology such as data warehousing, organizations will experience difficulties attracting and retaining skilled employees *and* contract workers (because vendors will be similarly affected by skill shortages). When working with third parties, success depends on clearly established lines of responsibility for plans, deliverables, due dates, and communications.

People Interviewed

Irvin Coleman, Jr., Business Systems Manager

Rita Fridman, Business Consultant

George C. Haettinger, Business Systems Manager

John K. Helmerci, Director, Finance and Human Resource Systems

Ken Nelson, Business Systems Manager, Corporate Division Systems

Brian Onufer, Associate Business Systems Manager

Dennis Pankow, Associate Business Systems Manager

MSC.Software

Company Profile

If you have ever watched Tiger Woods drive a golf ball, or if you have observed a plane land, an airbag deploy, or a bus brake for a pedestrian, you have witnessed the results of MSC.Software's products.[1] MSC.Software is the world's largest provider of mechanical, computer-aided engineering strategies, software, and services. MSC.Software's solutions—state-of-the-art technologies that combine mechanical engineering and computer science—have played a key role in the design of virtually every major automobile, aircraft, and space vehicle developed in the past decade. The 1998 Annual Report states:

> Simply, we enable our customers to design and build better products faster. We do this with computer-aided engineering software and services. We minimize the need for costly prototypes and time-consuming tests with computer simulations of product performance and the manufacturing process.

MSC.Software is the largest single provider of finite element analysis (FEA) products. FEA is an analytical method engineers use to help determine how well structural designs survive in actual conditions such as stress, vibration, heat, and other forces. FEA operates on the premise that a complex structure can be divided into smaller elements to form a finite-element model simulating the structure's physical properties. The model is subjected to rigorous mathematical analysis, and the results can be reviewed in a variety of formats. FEA significantly reduces the time and costs associated with prototyping and physical testing.

Headquartered in Los Angeles, California, MSC.Software is organized around core customer groups:

- The Aerospace group, the oldest and most important market segment, focuses on enabling customers to optimize their design-to-certification process.

- The Automotive group, which supports the popular design anywhere, build anywhere philosophy, focuses on customers' key disciplines: noise, vibration, and harshness; durability; occupant safety; and vehicle dynamics.

- The Growth Industries group helps customers (including such diverse companies as Bausch & Lomb, Fender Guitars, General Electric, Harley Davidson, Hewlett-Packard, Intel, and Qualcomm) verify their designs early in the process and reduce potential product warranty and liability costs.

- International Operations provides state-of-the-art products and services to businesses in Europe and Asia-Pacific.

Two characteristics related to the engineering focus of its business distinguish the organizational culture of MSC.Software. First, many senior executives and managers come from engineering backgrounds. Second, it has no typical customers. Customers range from huge corporations (e.g., automobile manufacturers and aerospace companies) to small, entrepreneurial operations (e.g., a start-up golf club manufacturer). MSC.Software's solutions are used to verify traditional as well as trend-setting and state-of-the-art product designs.

Precursors to the Data Warehouse

Software has been one of MSC.Software's primary FEA products. The accounting requirements related to software revenue recognition magnified the inadequacies of MSC.Software's legacy financial systems, setting the stage for the decision to implement a data warehouse.

Revenue Recognition

The company's FEA software is primarily leased rather than purchased, and leasing complicates both revenue recognition and commission calculations. Further complicating matters, the software is often packaged with third-party hardware and/or software platform products, requiring royalty payments. Timing the recognition of revenue and calculating the corresponding commissions and royalties are challenging. According to CFO Lou Greco, "Everything else about this company is vanilla. Revenue accounting is the most unique I've come across."

Software revenue consists of licensing fees, which are charged for the right to use the software, and maintenance fees, which provide for support and upgrade privileges. Software license revenue and maintenance fees account for over 90 percent of MSC.Software's total revenues, which were approximately $135 million for the year ending January 31, 1998.

MSC.Software recognizes software revenue in accordance with the AICPA's Statement of Position (SOP) 91-1, *Software Revenue Recognition,* issued in 1991.[2] Revenues are recognized in four ways:

- Revenues from monthly leases of computer software products are recognized as invoiced and earned.

- A portion of revenues from prepaid and paid-up licenses is recognized in the month of invoice, and the remainder is spread over the license term.

- Revenues for paid-up licenses are recognized as invoiced.

- Revenues associated with support and upgrade privileges for paid-up licenses are spread ratably over the term of the license agreement.

Revenues from the sales of products provided by third-party suppliers (where royalties are due) are reported as gross revenues earned from the product sales. Royalties due to the suppliers represent an operating expense and are recorded as royalty expense in cost of revenue. Service and other revenues are recognized when the service is provided and the revenue has been earned. Long-term contracts are recognized using the percentage of completion method.

MSC.Software's executives and managers monitor revenues by industry and by product, and revenues are reported four different ways:

■ *Invoiced*—Invoiced revenues are based on the date the invoice was generated (e.g., revenues could be invoiced in one year and earned in another). These revenue reports are especially useful for cash-flow analysis.

■ *Sales*—Sales revenues are based on the date the license agreement was completed. Sales revenues will be identical to invoiced revenues except when a customer is paying in multiple installments (e.g., monthly billing rather than annual billing). These revenue reports are useful for understanding the sales and renewal cycles.

■ *GAAP*—GAAP (generally accepted accounting procedures) revenues are based on the GAAP rules for revenue recognition. These official numbers are used for external reporting and are reviewed by senior management and the board of directors.

■ *Earned*—Earned revenues reflect the perfect world—without delays in contract signing or invoicing. These revenue reports are used by marketing personnel as an accurate picture of revenues. Commissions are usually based on earned revenues.

Legacy Financial Systems

MSC.Software's legacy financial systems, early versions of packaged software, were inadequate for revenue accounting. The revenue accounting module had a manufacturing (rather than a leasing) focus.

In 1991 MSC.Software arranged with Oracle to install early versions of its packaged financial software modules. Still under development, these software modules included general ledger, accounts payable, accounts receivable, fixed assets, and revenue accounting. MSC.Software's management thought that Oracle was developing the revenue accounting module for use in its own software business, which was closely aligned with MSC.Software's business.

However, during the nine months that elapsed before delivery, Oracle's revenue module was changed from a leasing focus to a manufacturing focus in order to satisfy the requirements of an important Oracle customer. As Lou Greco explained:

At the time, Oracle was the only one with a complete financial package like this. All other parts of the package were a good fit, especially with our recent acquisitions. So we went ahead with it.

To address the immediate shortcomings of the revenue accounting module, MSC.Software's internal IS department developed a custom software module for lease maintenance that interfaced with the other packaged modules. But this was just an interim solution. The lease maintenance module functioned as a stopgap measure to capture revenue data.

Revenue reporting was, at best, cumbersome. Analysts in Finance did quarterly top-side accruals with spreadsheets. These top-side accruals (e.g., resulting from billing delays or changes to revenue recognition policies) had to be added to the invoiced, earned, and GAAP revenues. Thus, the revenue reports did not match the general ledger. Dan Bryce, Chief Information Officer (CIO), described the revenue reports three years ago, before the data warehouse was implemented:

The month-end reports were "birdcage paper." There were 30 or 40 revenue reports, and they didn't add up. Nothing matched. It drove the CEO nuts. The CFO complained that the reports didn't show him anything!

Senior executives were not the only ones complaining. Analysts in the IS department found the situation intolerable, too.

One reason was the time-consuming and labor-intensive nature of the month-end reporting process. The reports took numerous hours to print. And even though the reports were voluminous, analysts in the IS department were inundated every month with requests for additional, customized reports. Julie Gutierrez, Database Analyst in the IS department, described the situation:

The month-end reports were a foot high, and printing would take forever. In addition, we did 25 custom reports to add such things as documentation revenues and consulting revenues. We had three to four people in IS just working on reports. We were drowning! We had users who wanted help. They wanted the data reformatted—

italics, left justified, right justified, portrait, landscape, move this over, round off totals, etc. The printer would get jammed. I'd have to unjam the printer and reprint. Formatting things would take forever. The report-writing tools were difficult. It was not fun—it was miserable working here. Now [with the warehouse] we can keep pace with the changes they're requesting.

The added burden of reconciliation also frustrated the IS analysts. Because of the inadequacies of the systems, individual workgroups kept their own databases. Sales people, for example, kept track of commissions. These workgroups expected IS to reconcile the differences among the databases.

Advent of the Multidimensional Revenue Datamart

Eventually, the concept of a data mart emerged. The data mart came to be known as MRD (Multidimensional Revenue Datamart). Lou Greco credits Dan Bryce for the idea.

Dan brought the data warehouse concept to us. Everyone was asking for data. We were producing 20 to 40 hard-coded reports. Dan suggested a data mart and put together a proposal package in layman's terms: What would a data mart do for us? How many people were needed? What was required? The proposal was only a few slides. Then I attended an E&Y [Ernst and Young] seminar on data warehouses and data marts. But we were beyond where E&Y was at the time. We took the proposal to the CEO, and the CEO said okay. Dan went off and built it; he did a lot of the work himself.

Dan Bryce told us:

The CEO said "go fix it." We didn't need to get him on board. At that time we were just scrambling. We had barely enough people to keep going. The initial effort to get MRD up and running was three people working for six months. A separate effort, which took seven months and turned out to be a dead end, was to fix the existing reports.

The initial goals of the data-mart project were as follows:

1. Improve the accuracy and completeness of the revenue reports.

2. Reduce the time required to generate the reports by removing the reporting burden from the production systems.

3. Reduce the support effort for IS analysts, and enable the users to be self-sufficient.

The Design of MRD

The initial design delivered immediate benefits, unlike many data warehouse implementations. According to Julie Gutierrez, "When we implemented MRD, we got rid of 25 reports on one day!"

Requirements Analysis

To accelerate the implementation of MRD, the IS department designers identified what information users requested most frequently. The IS department did its own requirements analysis without explicit user involvement. Julie Gutierrez said:

> We didn't do JAD [joint application development], RAD [rapid application development], or anything like that. We just looked at what they [the users] were getting before and just made those things, and more, available.

The designers made the MRD information readily available to users (e.g., analysts and clerks from accounting, marketing, finance, and billing) in predefined models at an intranet site. Users could customize the predefined models by selecting settings for parameters such as invoice dates, regions, and products. Then, using simple, point-and-click menu selections, users could query and download data without slowing the production systems and could format reports using familiar tools—Excel and pivot tables.

Technical Design

The initial technical design was straightforward. Relevant data from the Oracle modules and from the custom-built module were housed offline on a Hewlett-Packard platform—separate from the production systems.

(Before MRD, the old-style reports were cumbersome, and IS analysts had to run them on the production systems.) The feeder systems (sources of MRD data) are summarized in table 6.1.

Two important components of the technical design made MRD inherently user friendly. First was the use of an intranet site. Users retrieved data from a Web site, something they were already comfortable doing. Second was the use of Excel as the desktop spreadsheet. Users retrieved data and populated an Excel spreadsheet with pivot tables. Again, users were already comfortable with Excel. These two design considerations contributed to the business units' rapid acceptance of MRD.

The Evolution of MRD

MRD's capabilities have evolved and grown over time. Since its inception, MRD has been an expanding and evolving work in progress. "It's always changing," according to Julie Gutierrez. When we asked Lou Greco if he was satisfied, he responded, "I couldn't ask for more! The challenge now is getting international data into it."

Table 6.1
Summary of MRD Feeder Systems

Module	Key Information Provided	Comments
Accounts Receivable (Oracle legacy module)	■ Invoices, including sales representative and territory ■ Some accruals	A/R system closes by month, so top-side accruals are not included
Lease Maintenance Module (custom built in-house)	■ Sales representative reassignments ■ Top-side accruals ■ Reconciliation to move revenue from one period to another	Top-side accruals are done monthly (originally they were done quarterly)
Order Entry/ Inventory (Oracle legacy module)	Shipping information	

Data Additions

To reflect the changing business environment, both data and capabilities have been added. Some examples of changes to the data include:

- *Reorganizing the data*—When MSC.Software eliminated its Central Region, the data had to be reorganized.

- *Increasing the level of detail*—When detail below the product level was included in the general ledger, changes had to be made to MRD.

- *Adding new data*—Information was added to MRD to distinguish "assigned" sales representatives and "actual" revenue sales representatives since they were not always the same. Other recent additions included data from Europe (e.g., internal company data from European operations, currency conversion rates, tax information, and postal codes).

Data Cleanup

As MRD evolved and usage grew, the biggest problem turned out to be "dirty" data. The data needed to be cleaned. For example, Standard Industry Codes (SICs) identifying customers were, at times, inconsistent. An unspecified SIC field might have been entered as a randomly selected SIC or as TBD (to be determined). Customers' addresses were sometimes incorrect. An address in Ontario, Canada, might have been entered as Ontario, California. To correct these problems and instill confidence in the data, MSC.Software undertook a major effort to clean up the data. After the cleanup, processes and procedures were put in place to ensure the ongoing quality of the data.

Training and Support

Getting employees to understand and use a new technology is always a challenge. And data-warehouse technology has an added challenge—getting employees to understand the data. Understanding and interpreting the data are often the most difficult lessons of training.

When MRD was introduced, the IS department provided the initial training. According to Julie Gutierrez, "Dan [Bryce] was a champion.

He gave the classes himself to the financial executives. I did some demos in the marketing department. Users reacted positively."

Harris Hunt, Director, Business Processes, who serves as a roving technology ambassador, has provided subsequent MRD training. An introductory MRD training session runs about 90 minutes with 10 vuegraphs. The training includes an overview of data marts, an explanation of how a data mart applies to MSC.Software, a demonstration of examples, a review of Excel and Excel pivot tables, and the distribution of a crib sheet. About half of the training session emphasizes the importance of understanding data-related questions to be asked and answered using MRD. A sample marketing question might be, How many customers have products that are three years old and need purchased upgrades? After the class, Hunt follows up with participants and reports that "people get pretty excited over the tools."

Security and Controls

Appropriate levels of security and controls have evolved with the growth of MRD. Employees sign a nondisclosure agreement, and approvals are required by three gatekeepers: one for computer accounts, one for MRD access, and one for MRD training. Audit trails are maintained and reviewed periodically by internal audit.

User-Requested Enhancements

The user community has requested some changes, and the IS department has requested others. Lou Greco highlighted the ease of enhancements. "Either MRD was designed in a flexible way, or there's a little elf there. We ask Dan for something not there, and 24 hours later it appears. It must be the design flexibility!"

User-initiated change requests are submitted through the help desk or the user forum conference, a regularly scheduled meeting of IS people and users. Greg Bryan, Corporate Controller, confirms that "the user forum meets regularly, and they're pretty detail oriented." The user forum systematically reviews the status of new, ongoing, and completed change requests. MRD change-request status information is also posted on an intranet site accessible to interested employees who do not attend the forum meeting. Julie Gutierrez noted, "We keep track of requests. Report 21 is the most frequently requested."

Operational Enhancements

The success of MRD prompted the IS department to initiate some operational improvements. Once users converted to MRD, they became dependent on it. They also became intolerant of response-time degradation and/or routine-maintenance downtime.

To satisfy the user community, the IS department implemented two data marts with a seamless changeover process (eliminating downtime) and moved the rebuild off to a separate machine (improving performance). MRD is completely rebuilt every two weeks. Offloading data from the production systems takes 30 minutes twice a week, and the rebuild takes seven to eight hours. But now, regardless of the maintenance cycle, response times for reporting are always less than five minutes.

Note: Periodically rebuilding a data warehouse is not the norm. Most data warehouses have detailed and summarized data added at regular intervals, but the entire warehouse is not rebuilt. However, this rebuild process works well for MSC.Software because of the manageable size of MRD. The periodic rebuild process has provided a convenient mechanism to implement changes in response to needs of the rapidly changing business environment. These changes have included reorganizing the data, increasing the level of detail, and adding new data. Because the rebuild is done routinely, the changeover process to an updated warehouse is smooth and seamless.

Benefits of MRD

Benefits of MRD include the prompt availability of information, the formatting of reports according to user preferences, and a reduction in the time IS analysts require to provide revenue reporting services. Some of the benefits were realized immediately, while others took time to evolve.

More Accurate and Timely Revenue Reports

One of the obvious benefits of MRD is prompt, accurate, and consistent revenue reporting. MRD is used routinely to calculate sales commissions and royalties. Recently, sales forecasting capabilities were added. Mas Matsumoto, Assistant Controller, highlighted the reporting benefits:

> MRD has improved efficiency and consistency. Reports that used to take 10 hours[3] are now available in minutes, and anybody worldwide can run a report and get the same result. We review many different revenue reports a day—by SIC, by product line, by third party vendors, for consulting by region and industry, etc. An added benefit has been that our knowledge of Excel has improved.

Consistent and Accurate Data

Before MRD, data entry was done at corporate headquarters in Los Angeles, which received paper from the field. Business units in the field kept their own sets of records, which did not always match the records at corporate. Lou Greco explained the problem. "It's 'corporate's data.' It's not mine, it's yours. Now [with MRD] data entry is done in the field, and they 'own' the data."

Users in the field trust the data because they entered and own the data. If something appears to be incorrect, they do a "reasonableness" check and correct any errors. In addition, the reconciliation process has been eliminated because commissions are paid using MRD.

Dan Bryce emphasized, "The quality of the data is a key risk. It's important to sell people in the field on the idea of entering it correctly." Therefore, before field order-entry was implemented, managers were brought to Los Angeles to learn the system. Then Harris Hunt conducted on-site training sessions in the field. Ruth Robbins, Manager of Automotive Finance and Administration, articulated the success of this approach. She arranged for Harris Hunt to give training sessions to her unit in Detroit and reported that field entry in her unit has resulted in more accurate data.

Better Decisions

Lou Greco reported:

> We use MRD for everything now—sales commissions, incentives, royalties, revenues by region and business unit, sales forecasting, etc. Now that management is confident and relying on data, our decisions are better. We get better partnering arrangements [with

hardware and software suppliers]. We can produce revenue reports by options within a product. We know what industries and what companies have bought what options.

Revenue data can be analyzed by product and options, by industry, by geographic region, or by hardware/software platform. Management can better determine which products and options are the most profitable and where investments in product development will yield the highest returns.

Reduced Workload on IS Analysts

By shifting responsibility to the users, MRD has reduced the support effort for IS analysts and has enabled the users to be more self-sufficient. Julie Gutierrez noted:

They have to run the reports with the right parameters, and they are responsible. There is a help desk. We used to get a lot of calls—some people called me or Dan directly. Now they help each other, and they train the new people.

The three to four IS analysts who used to spend time customizing revenue reports or reconciling workgroups' databases are now freed up for other IS department projects.

Organizational Agility

One of the unexpected benefits of MRD is the ability to reconfigure the organization and change the reporting structure to meet changing business needs. MRD can be used to do "as of" reporting. For example, invoices from several years ago could still be generating revenues, which need to be reported. Due to changes in the organizational structure, the original organizational units that received the revenues may have changed, and the revenues need to be reported to a new organizational unit as of a particular date.

Proactive Infrastructure Planning

As the use of MRD has grown, the requirements for data communications bandwidth have increased. Many users downloading data from MRD with Web browsers can stress the communications infrastructure.

One of the side benefits of MRD has been to serve as an early-warning system, alerting management to the data communications bandwidth issue and forcing proactive infrastructure planning and expansion.

Other Business Opportunities

Following the success of MRD, MSC.Software developed another data mart—an installation data mart with detailed customer data by product and by platform. One customer (e.g., a large automobile manufacturer or a multinational corporation) could have MSC.Software's products installed on several hundred different computers with numerous hardware and software platform configurations. Different divisions of a customer company could deal with different MSC.Software sales representatives.

The installation data mart tracks these complexities. It includes detailed information tied to different levels of a customer relationship: agreement, host machine (e.g., operating system, version, billing address, shipping address), installation (e.g., product, lease status, support status, sales representatives with percentages), and options (e.g., billing data and beginning and ending dates). Marketing and Development use data and trends from the installation data mart to make investment decisions on products and hardware/software platforms. For example, an analyst could identify strong growth in the sales of a particular MSC.Software product within an industry when the product is packaged with a specific third-party hardware/software platform. Then, based on growth projections for the industry, Development could decide to invest resources to enhance product functions for that industry or third-party platform.

Without the previous success of MRD, MSC.Software probably would not have undertaken developing the installation data mart.

Key Success Factors

From the perspectives of senior management, the business units, and the IS department, MRD has been a success. But why has MSC.Software been successful while many organizations that have attempted data-mart projects either failed or abandoned their efforts? The key factors are summarized on the following pages.

Satisfy a Pressing Business Need

MSC.Software had a pressing business need: timing the recognition of revenue and calculating the corresponding commissions and royalties for leased software using inadequate, legacy financial information systems.

Revenue recognition and reporting had to be done, and the IS department was barely able to keep up with the demands. Thus, from the IS department's viewpoint, MRD was a necessity rather than an option. The IS department—not the business units—initiated MRD, and IS did it for survival reasons. Julie Gutierrez explained, "We didn't do cost justification or any ROI [return on investment] calculations. This was survival!"

Use Empathic Design and Build It Quickly

The IS department employed empathic design to build its data warehouse quickly.

> The techniques of empathic design—gathering, analyzing, and applying information gleaned from observation in the field—are familiar to top engineering/design companies and to a few forward-thinking manufacturers, but they are not common practice (p. 104).[4]

Empathic design may be particularly applicable to new information technologies where customers may unconsciously provide examples but often cannot articulate their needs. In these cases, observation of real behavior (rather than reported behavior) by a knowledgeable observer can identify unarticulated needs; and innovative IS people with an understanding of the business can be particularly effective and efficient. Dan Bryce described how the IS department took on the task:

> We worked with consultants initially. They suggested building a data warehouse. But they couldn't describe it, and they couldn't identify the benefits. So we did it internally. We understood it. The IS staff understands the business and the users. We don't rely on users to tell us what to do—we just do our job. We understand what the business users need—we have to. Sometimes they can't tell you. We have very sharp, high-quality people in IS.

Keep the Interface Simple and Use Familiar Tools

Greg Bryan summarized this key success factor: "Dan keeps it simple with Excel as the retrieval system." The IS department learned this lesson the hard way—the first warehouse attempt failed. According to Julie Gutierrez:

> It was a star schema with Business Objects as a front-end tool. It was too complicated. The terminology was an issue with our financial people. They prefer using Excel, which has been a key to MRD's success.

The simplicity of the interface is elegant. Users customize predefined models. We saw numerous examples of people who were able to learn and use MRD quickly.

Brenda Devina, a Financial Analyst who had been with MSC.Software for six months, uses MRD for commissions and other analyses. "Just about everyone in Finance uses MRD. I'm not a computer guru— I don't understand the intricacies. I just run reports." She showed us how easy MRD was to use. She chose a report from the menu, set some parameters related to dates and areas, and requested that a report be sent in a file via e-mail. The report arrived within minutes. She saved the file and opened it with Excel. A pivot table was already set up.

Cathy Okuni, a Financial Analyst who had been with MSC.Software for about one year, uses MRD for royalties and commissions for resellers. She also helps prepare the management and board books.

> I like to play with computers. I can pick it up pretty easily. The MIS [management information systems] people are very helpful and very fast. If I want a new field in a report, they will add it. I called the help desk and asked them to add sales rep to a report. It took 24 hours for MIS to make the change.

Ensure Data Quality and Establish Data Ownership

MSC.Software built the warehouse first and then cleaned up the data. Once MRD was built and analysts began using it, the data became a credibility issue. The data needed to be consistent. Mas Matsumoto explained, "Everyone looks at the validity of the data. Belief in the system is very important."

In conjunction with cleaning the data, establishing ownership of the data is critical to ensure ongoing success. Everyone at MSC.Software emphasized the importance of data ownership. But data-related issues are frequently underestimated by organizations embarking on a warehouse project. Lou Greco cautions, "Data issues are at least 70 percent to 80 percent of the warehousing effort. Make sure these issues aren't underestimated, and make sure someone owns the data."

Let the Design Evolve

An IS department culture that is receptive to evolving designs is an important success factor. MRD became somewhat of a rapid prototype as the requirements evolved. The IS department did not hand off MRD when it was built. Instead, key people in the IS department maintained ongoing involvement.

Have an Evangelist with Credibility

The CIO, who used to be involved in the development of one of the engineering tools, came from product design and had a long history with MSC.Software. In a company dominated by engineers, Dan Bryce's credibility was firmly established before the MRD project. He became somewhat of an evangelist for MRD. He personally conducted the initial training sessions and responded to many of the early help desk calls.

When asked what advice he would give others who may be thinking about undertaking a data warehouse, Lou Greco said, "Get a Dan—but don't get Dan! Dan's a superman and a magician."

People Interviewed

Deepak Brar, Manager, Database Applications

Greg Bryan, Corporate Controller

Daniel Bryce, Ph.D., Chief Information Officer

Brenda E. Devina, Financial Analyst II

Louis A. Greco, Chief Financial Officer

Juliette Gutierrez, Database Analyst

Harris Hunt, Director, Business Processes

M. Mas Matsumoto, CPA, Assistant Controller

Annette McCusker, Unix Systems Administrator

Cathy K. Okuni, Financial Analyst

Rosendo "Don" Raymundo, Senior Staff Accountant

Ruth A. Robbins, Manager, Automotive Finance and Administration

Raj Sain, Manager, Revenue Accounting

Endnotes

1. Company profile information is from The MacNeal-Schwendler Corporation 1998 Annual Report and the MSC Web site at www.macsch.com.

2. In October 1997, the AICPA issued SOP 97-2, *Software Revenue Recognition,* which supercedes SOP 91-1. This method distinguishes between significant and insignificant vendor obligations as a basis for recording revenue, with a requirement that each element of a software licensing arrangement be separately identified and accounted for based on relative fair values of each element. MSC adopted SOP 97-2 in the first quarter of fiscal 1999.

3. Before MRD, about one hour of CPU time (equivalent to about four elapsed hours) was required to run a revenue report. The IS department's MRD goal of reducing CPU time to five minutes (equivalent to about 20 elapsed minutes) was achieved quickly. After several revisions to the reporting system, the IS department was able to reduce CPU time to one to two minutes so that users receive their requested information in less than five minutes.

4. Dorothy Leonard and Jeffrey F. Rayport. "Spark Innovation Through Empathic Design," *Harvard Business Review* 75, no. 6 (November–December 1997): 102–113.

Cardinal Health, Inc.

Case Summary

As a national wholesale distribution company, Cardinal Health relies heavily on IT to process customers' orders and assist customers' inventory management of pharmaceutical products. Since its beginning in 1979, the company has grown rapidly through the acquisition of regional wholesalers, each with its own unique operating philosophies and information systems.

- The first use of data warehousing at Cardinal was directed at systems consolidation to enable the company to present a single face to its national customers.

- A second use of data warehousing was directed at management reporting and decision support. A byproduct of Cardinal's intermediary position between pharmaceutical manufacturers and hospital and pharmacy customers is a vast quantity of information that could potentially be mined for value-added products and services.

- A third use of data warehousing was to develop new information products into new revenue sources.

Company Profile

Cardinal Health began in 1979 when a small, regional food distributor made its first acquisition in the drug wholesaling business. (Drug distribution was viewed as a promising business line since consolidation was just starting to occur, whereas consolidation in the grocery business was well advanced.) Over the next 15 years, the company grew into a national wholesaling concern through 15 horizontal acquisitions. Today, the distribution company has approximately $14 billion in annual sales and 19 percent market share. It ranks third in the industry behind McKesson Corp. and Bergen Brunswig Corp. The Federal Trade Commission rejected Cardinal's proposed acquisition of Bergen Brunswig on antitrust grounds.

As consolidation in the drug distribution business progressed, companies in the industry faced intense and increasing pressure on margins and profitability. For example, in 1980, Cardinal had gross margins of 11 percent and operating profits of 8 percent. In 1996, Cardinal had gross margins of 6 percent. The company was able to maintain a 3 percent operating profit by cutting its costs from 8 percent to 3 percent. (Today, the company sells to many hospital buying groups at prices below cost. Its operating profit from distribution activities comes from forward buying contracts and from cash discounts on purchases.)

In 1994, Cardinal Health began the second phase of its expansion. Having established itself as a national wholesaler, Cardinal began a program of diversification, again through acquisition. As a result of these acquisitions, it has become a pharmaceutical services company. Cardinal is now involved in automated pharmaceutical dispensing, hospital pharmacy management, hospital supplies, pharmacy franchising, and a number of new information businesses.

IT and Cardinal Health

Information processing is a core business function in wholesaling companies. Wholesalers differentiate themselves on the basis of price, quality of service (order processing speed and accuracy), geographic coverage, and breadth of product line; IT enables the core business activities of wholesalers and supports their efforts to manage costs and information.

Not surprisingly, Cardinal has invested heavily in IT. Since the mid-1980s, the company has been an industry leader in cost-effective information systems to support customers. Hospitals and independent pharmacies use IT products developed by Cardinal to place orders and manage inventories. For example, customers can use Cardinal-

CHOICE™ as a basic electronic item catalog and order entry system or as a complete inventory management system with economical order quantity procurement, interdepartmental billing, and electronic data interchange interfaces to a wide variety of other information systems. The next generation of CardinalCHOICE™ will be Internet enabled. CardinalCHOICE-HQ™ is a group purchasing reporting system designed for customers with multiple facilities. This technology presents data about all purchases from Cardinal by all the facilities of a customer in a single format. The customer can use this information to analyze purchase histories along a number of dimensions. (A data warehouse of invoice information drives this customer analysis and reporting function.)

Supporting Cardinal's customer information systems is a state-of-the art wide area network using the Internet protocol to tie all the company's IT resources into a single national information system. Implementation of this network began in 1996. Today, the network ties together two major corporate and five regional data centers for the distribution company and the subsidiaries. Cardinal was the first national pharmaceutical distributor to deploy an Internet-compatible network.

The first data warehousing initiative at Cardinal Health began in 1995 when Phil Greth, Cardinal's new Chief Information Officer, began the task of consolidating the diverse information systems of the different distribution companies acquired to make Cardinal into a national distribution company. Subsequent data warehousing initiatives were undertaken to support internal and customer decisionmaking and to develop new information-based products and services for sale by Cardinal Health subsidiaries.

The Uses of Data Warehousing at Cardinal Health

This section describes three groups of data warehousing initiatives at Cardinal Health. The first two groups are initiatives of the distribution company—the first aimed at systems consolidation and the second at decision support. The third was initiated within the distribution company but handed over to a new subsidiary—Cardinal Information Corporation—for further development and marketing.

Systems Integration

Before its 1994 merger with Whitmire Drug Company, Cardinal had 13 large distribution centers, primarily in the eastern half of the United States. Having started as independent companies, these centers were entrepreneurial and highly autonomous. According to Don Lyle, Director of Customer Support Services for National Accounts, "We called them the 13 colonies." Each distribution center maintained its own customer records, inventory management systems (including its own product item numbering scheme), and pricing policies.

Clearly, this local autonomy hindered Cardinal's ability to work with large customers who were supplied by several distribution centers. Cardinal undertook various integration efforts. For example, a new seven-digit centralized product numbering scheme was introduced. But the Whitmire merger made systems integration a major corporate agenda.

Unlike Cardinal, Whitmire was a highly centralized company, so it already had standardized customer accounts, product numbers, pricing policies, and so forth. (Whitmire also brought to the merger the pharmacy management software that later became known as Cardinal-CHOICE-HQ™.) But its product numbers differed from Cardinal's, and it used a different IT platform (HP, whereas Cardinal used IBM). All told, the new company had 11 different distribution management systems in 1995.

This lack of integration posed problems for Cardinal's largest customers. Some had formerly been customers of both Cardinal and Whitmire. They now expected to be able to deal with Cardinal as a unified entity. Instead, they found that two different distribution centers were charging them different prices for the same product. Further, Cardinal had difficulty giving them consolidated information on their total purchases from Cardinal. Because of the differences in technology and data formats, simply merging data from different systems didn't work. Each customer required custom-coded COBOL programs that took up to two months to write. Even then, Cardinal's reports were often incorrect. Since customers use information from pharmaceutical wholesalers to manage their inventories and costs, incomplete and inaccurate data were unacceptable. The poor quality of its information environment put Cardinal's national accounts at risk.

When Phil Greth was hired as the first CIO, he brought with him a vision of integrated information systems. What he found were sales and operations groups that each wanted to keep doing things the same way and a political struggle over whether IBM or HP was the platform of choice. He quickly put an end to the latter squabbles by deciding that the company would operate, in the intermediate term, two separate IT environments, despite the costs this might entail. Instead, he concentrated on integrating data and the company's interfaces with its customers. A common order receiving and routing system was developed to capture customers' orders from a variety of sources and to distribute them to the appropriate distribution center. Over time, the company consolidated the 11 different distribution management systems down to two. Now, five years later, the company is finally revisiting the two-environment decision with plans to make its IBM-hosted distribution management system a companywide standard. In the interim, achieving integration of data and business processes required much work. Said Greth:

> When I arrived, IT was getting lots of flak from the business: "Why can't you tell the customers what they are buying from us?" I get defensive when I hear these criticisms. Technology is not the major barrier to getting a company's data correct.

So, in 1995, Greth assembled a team of representatives of business units throughout the company. The IDEAS team was charged with recommending ways to achieve integration of business processes and data. The team quickly concluded that it would be necessary to manage customer account data, product item data, contract and pricing data, and sales/invoice databases centrally. This, in turn, would require major changes in the company's systems and business practices.

The first enterprise integration effort the IDEAS team initiated was the Central Pricing System (CPS), implemented in late 1996. This system was designed to ensure control over the pricing policies applied to customers' orders before the orders were forwarded to the two distribution management systems. Currently, this system is being completely redesigned to take maximum advantage of later IT developments, described below.

7

The second IDEAS-initiated project was a corporate sales data warehouse, known as CSD (for Corporate Sales Database). Phil Greth said:

I told the IS folks that they had to get a data warehouse working in six months for a cost of $1 million. It cost twice as much and took 14 months to build, but I thought that was wonderful. A competitor that built a similar system got enamored of the latest technology and spent in excess of $10 million.

This warehouse was to contain 24 months of sales invoice data, derived from the then 11 different distribution management systems. Local operations initially did not want to use the central database, preferring their own data sources, even though these same sources fed the warehouse. They claimed not to trust corporate data. The IDEAS team recognized that reconciling CSD data with the general ledger would be essential to establishing the legitimacy of the data.

When the warehouse was first loaded in 1996, agreement with the general ledger was very poor—off by millions of dollars. In some cases, return authorizations were not being credited. Some invoices were double counted; others were omitted. A team of finance specialists systematically analyzed and corrected sources of error in the data over a period of six months until the warehoused data agreed with the general ledger to within 0.01 percent. The warehouse, which ran on an AS/400 platform, was fully operational by June 1998.

According to Richard Miller, Corporate Vice President and Controller, CSD now provides much more detail than the general ledger. Whereas the ledger groups sales into five customer classes, CSD now provides sales data by customer, enabling financial specialists to answer such questions as "What is the level of business of the top 20 independent pharmacies?" Or "Why is the independent segment up 22 percent?" Today, the CSD is being expanded so it can meet the decision support needs of both Cardinal's employees and customers. Access to the warehouse is gained via the company intranet.

A third initiative stemming from the IDEAS team was the creation of a master item file (MIF) to provide common numbering and descriptions of products Cardinal sells. According to Scott Summers, Manager, Customer Systems Marketing, and Dave Blickensderfer, Manager, Software Development for Customer Information Systems, initial attempts to solve this problem with cross-reference tables didn't work. "The match would link a certain product packaged in a quantity of one with the same product packaged in a quantity of 10. It was a nightmare—it was ugly." The solution was to develop a centralized product database to feed the two different distribution management systems. This solution required duplicate data entry for a time, but, with the ultimate unification of the distribution management system, these redundancies will be eliminated.

Rather than adopt either of the two product numbering schemes then in place, Cardinal adopted a scheme that was developed and is maintained by a leading third-party data provider to the pharmaceutical warehousing industry. The first phase of the MIF project, completed in mid-1997, involved supplying consistent descriptions and pricing information for 150,000 items. A second phase (planned for end 1999) is extending the volume of information about each item. The result of this initiative has been much more accurate reporting to customers about contract compliance, especially concerning policies on the use of generic product equivalents.

A fourth integration effort traceable to the IDEAS project team was the development of the customer data warehouse, called CCDB (central customer database). Before CCDB was deployed in mid-1998, no central source provided customer data; each distribution center maintained its own information. Because of understandable differences in the definition of a customer's "ship to" address—the hospital, parent organization, or buying group—and because of rapid changes owing to mergers and changes in hospital buying group membership, Cardinal had difficulty achieving an accurate picture of national and regional accounts. CCDB was designed to provide people throughout Cardinal with a single consistent data source on these larger customers.

Some of the information in CCDB comes from a third-party database of information about hospitals. People in the field provide other data. To ensure data integrity, a team within the Sales organization was set up to handle account maintenance for customers that use two or more distribution centers. (Field personnel can access the data but not update them.) Special data entry screens simplify the setup and maintenance of multilocation accounts.

In summary, two data warehouses, CSD (more accurately called an operational data store) and CCDB played a prominent role in Cardinal

Health's efforts to integrate the operations of acquired business units. In addition, these warehouses support customer and internal decisionmaking.

Decision Support

In the early 1980s, Ronald Morgan, Cardinal Distribution's Senior Vice President for Information Systems, worked at Northwest Industries when Ben Heinemann was CEO. Heinemann was the subject of a widely read *Harvard Business Review* article (Rockart and Treacy, 1982) for his hands-on use of computer-based decision support technology. So, when Ronald Morgan came to Cardinal, he said:

> I felt like I'd taken a 15-year leap backward in one fell swoop. Our decision support environment here was that bad. It took me six months to find someone with the background to do what we needed, and then it took him a year to build us a data environment with the three "A's": availability, actionability, and accuracy.

Today, Cardinal Health's intranet, called The Aviary (implemented in 1997) provides access to numerous internal data resources to support decisionmaking. Under the banner of Cardinal Health, Inc., information about Corporate Account Management can be found. Here authorized users access CCDB. Under the banner of Cardinal Distribution are three sites: Customer Information Systems, Distribution Operations, and Sales and Marketing Information.

Customer Information Systems

One of Cardinal's key services is providing information to enable customers to better manage their inventories. Until quite recently, the technological environment for providing reports and responding to customer queries was poor. Queries were run against operational databases at odd times to avoid reducing the performance of the core transaction systems. According to Gina Harrobin, Manager of Decision Support Systems for Customer Information Systems:

> We'd submit queries, and we were lucky to get a response within a week. It took three weeks to get sales data for a particular date range. It was ridiculous. We adopted the motto "easy access to useful information" and went to work, hiring a consultant to help us.

We didn't have users saying "We want a data warehouse." Higher ups in Information Systems decided data warehousing was the solution. We ended up having a number of debates with our consultants about this. They said "What's the business problem?" They wanted us to come up with projections on how much it would save us in terms of maintenance, etc. We didn't really care. We weren't even sure it would save us money. The technology was just so bad. People were screaming for reports. They needed immediate access to their information. IS couldn't move ahead strategically because we were bombarded with tactical requests.

Upper-level sales managers agreed with the IS philosophy that they would do their own report retrieval and query writing—a philosophy that dictated the choice of data analysis and access tools. IS proceeded to develop a quick solution. Said Gina Harrobin, "We didn't want to take two years to do the perfect data warehouse. Plus, the business is changing rapidly, which means the data structures would change."

Starting in 1997, IS made data from CSD available to a broader user group via the company's wide area network. The tool first chosen to support this use was the DSS/Agent ROLAP from MicroStrategy. During the pilot project, the limitations of this technology became apparent, and the DSS/Agent product was replaced with MicroStrategy's new Web-enabled tool. This technology was rolled out companywide in 1998.

While the warehouse has met with some success, there have been some disappointments. Harrobin said,

We did a presentation for a senior exec, who asked my boss, "Where are my such-and-such reports?" We realized that for some users, it wasn't a report until it was printed. We have about 20 users of our Web site now, but we expected more. The hurdles may be fear, may be cultural. We do lots of demos that go over really well. People say, "Wow, I can see the data from my hotel room now when I travel." But they still call an administrative assistant and ask her to fax them a hard-copy report.

Training does not entirely eliminate the problem. "We give two- and four-hour classes that worked well for some. But people who didn't know Access found it overwhelming. Now we're taking a one-on-one approach," said Harrobin.

Don Lyle, Director of Customer Support Services for National Accounts, is responsible for prioritizing requests for IT support. He understands the downside of the new decision support environment:

> Before, people used to get a lot of paper reports. Now, we're telling them, "Here are the data." I have to train my folks in Access to put the data into the format the customer wants.

In summary, Cardinal's data warehousing initiatives are making a huge difference in the quality of data and reports available to people in various business units. At the same time, the ability to make full use of the new information environment requires changes in managers' skills and habits.

Distribution Operations
Mike Proulx, Vice President of Operations, described how he went about developing a decision support system for the distribution company.

> In mid-1996, as a result of a strategy study, we got funding to develop a data warehouse to support operations. We surveyed managers about the information they needed to run the distribution business. They came back with a list of 158 measurements! Our base systems didn't even collect all the data needed to produce these measures. They also said, "Don't make us become programmers to use the thing—give us canned reports."

> So I decided that in Phase 1, we'd go after the top 29 metrics. My secret weapon in developing the data warehouse was a programmer who grew up in the [distribution] warehouse. He's able to translate both ways between the distribution folks and IT specialists.

Roughly 80 people, mostly financial analysts and general managers, use the Distribution data warehouse. Little training is required to use today's data warehouse; the "secret weapon" programmer provided whatever training was needed. Today, the warehouse provides access only to preformatted reports; users do not yet have the capability to drill down into the numbers to do in-depth analysis. Drill-down capability is an enhancement planned for Phase 2. Another next step is to score the divisions on their performance on 24 measures over the course of the year. The plan is to have this information available the next day so operations personnel can see the results of the previous day's performance. (Currently, information is available within eight days of the month-end rollup.) Achieving this goal will require some reverse engineering of the legacy applications to capture detailed transaction data at the level of distribution routes. Mike Proulx explained that his approach to decision support requires changing both systems and business processes in parallel.

> Systems can only maintain the consistency of your approach; they cannot do things for you. Ninety-nine percent of all improvement comes from the efforts of the operations guys. And to make improvements, they need good information. If you can't measure it, you can't improve it, you can't get better.

A clear lesson here is that getting business benefits from data warehousing may require changes in performance measurement and evaluation, or, in other words, the focus and style of management.

Sales and Marketing Information

Tracey Malone, Manager of Marketing Projects, is responsible for marketing research at Cardinal Health. This has been a challenging job for two reasons. First, the market is complex, with many customer segments and subgroups, and changing rapidly as hospitals and pharmacies merge into chains or otherwise change ownership. Second, until the development of CCDB in 1998, she was unable to aggregate sales data from CSD by customers across all the distribution centers. (Even today, high-quality third-party customer data are available only for hospitals; for the retail pharmacy segments, much less information is available.)

Working with an outside vendor, Tracey Malone and her boss, the Executive Vice President (EVP) of Corporate Accounts Management, initiated a data warehouse project to support marketing efforts to the hospital sector. Launched in third quarter 1998, the reaction of the approximately 20 users has been "How have we ever lived without this?" At the same time, Malone has concerns about rising expectations:

> This project may grow into my worst nightmare. Today, it only covers hospitals. People want it to cover the retail pharmacy segment, too. But we have horrible problems with data on retail. There are 35,000 to 40,000 independent pharmacies out there—a huge

customer base, very difficult to track. We've asked a third-party information provider to track retail pharmacies as they do hospitals, but they're undecided about whether to do this yet.

Use of the marketing database is restricted to the most senior levels of sales and marketing management and corporate executives, because the information is highly sensitive. While the warehouse is very user-friendly, the consultant who developed the warehouse is providing training.

Recently, Tracey Malone gave a presentation on the warehouse to a staff meeting of 150 attendees, using "Cardinal Jeopardy" as the theme. The top five vice presidents were asked to play a game in which they had to risk their own money to answer questions about their customer bases.

> I picked really obscure questions like "Who ranked 13th through 19th in your region during the first quarter of this year?" and "Which customer had the highest distribution in Decatur?" I didn't do the demo live: I'd preselected the questions and did screen prints of the answers from the warehouse. The presentation was very effective.

New Information Products

As drug wholesalers consolidated, so did hospitals' pharmaceutical buying patterns. Where they had formerly bought both from manufacturers and a variety of local distributors, they increasingly began merging into hospital chains with exclusive relationships with distributors or joining buying groups with other hospitals to achieve sizable purchasing discounts. Companies like Cardinal needed new ways to influence customers' purchasing decisions. Increasingly, Cardinal is finding new business opportunities in sharing information with customers and suppliers. One particular focus on information sharing lies in the area of health outcomes measurement.

Health outcomes measurement has been a goal of the health care industry for years. Outcomes measurement requires data from all parties in the pharmaceutical supply chain, from manufacturers to patients. By virtue of its intermediary role between manufacturers and prescribers/dispensers, Cardinal has a unique opportunity to collect data on health outcomes.

Pyxis is a key element in Cardinal's health outcomes measurement ventures. Acquired by Cardinal in 1996, Pyxis is the leading U.S. manufacturer of in-hospital automated drug dispensing systems. Pyxis machines are like drug automatic teller machines in hospital wards: They give hospitals much greater control over their inventories and usage. At the same time, these machines track medications use by patient. Combined with patient diagnostic data, Pyxis dispensing data are a powerful information asset. When Cardinal acquired MediQual Systems, Inc., in 1998, the cycle was complete. MediQual is a clinical information management company that specializes in hospital outcome studies.

Robert Zollars, EVP and Group President of Cardinal Health, described MediQual as "a data-mining company in search of data" and Cardinal as "a data company in search of someone to mine it and figure out what to do with it. ... There was an understanding ... that there was a lot of data we weren't doing much with" (quoted in Levin, 1998). Recognizing this gap, Phil Greth hired a consulting company to review Cardinal's IT assets and develop a plan to mine them. According to Fritz Krieger, Vice President/General Manager of Cardinal Information Corporation, that study recommended three new business opportunities. Two were rejected because they required acquiring companies with old legacy information systems "two and a half years before Y2K." Fritz Krieger was hired to pursue the third opportunity.

> I visited all my sister divisions and found some diamonds in the rough and a few ugly ducklings. I invited the 10 largest pharmaceutical firms to a weekend retreat, like a focus group. I shared our assets and potential product ideas. I learned that there was a lot of dissatisfaction in the industry with the products of current data providers [owing mainly to the quality of their technological infrastructure].

> I found two kinds of data needs. The first was for the same kind of data currently available, but with product preference features. People want data with greater currency and drill-down capability. We could win in this market by providing Web delivery of information with a faster refresh rate and more granularity. A second area of need was for data on what's going on within the hospital: How are

pharmaceuticals being used, by whom, with what outcomes? We thought we could get there, and Jericho™ was the result.

The outcomes data used in Jericho™ are automatically collected by specially modified Pyxis machines in hospitals that have granted Cardinal permission to collect the data. Cardinal believes that it must acquire clear ownership rights to data in order to have a viable long-term business model in the information product business. In return for their data, the hospitals gain access to Cardinal's value-added contribution: information about how well particular drugs do in treatment and institution-specific outcome information compared with results from other institutions. This information is far more extensive and detailed than that currently available from other sources. (Naturally, the value of this service depends on the number of participants.)

During Jericho's development, Fritz Krieger met with numerous hospitals. He learned, to his surprise, that what he'd thought was a product for manufacturers had a large potential market in hospitals. Hospitals were interested in using Jericho for internal assessment and improvement.

> Manufacturers get great value from Jericho, too. They can learn about the dosages physicians are prescribing and about off-label uses. If outcome data show that a particular drug is not the best for a given diagnosis, Jericho can find a population [of patients] for which the drug *is* best. This could revolutionize drug marketing.

Jericho's analytic engine is data warehousing technology. Hospitals and manufacturers query the data warehouse to produce the reports they need. By contrast, some competitive offerings provide only summarized data in preformatted paper reports. Detailed analyses, when possible, require the analyst to rekey the data into an analysis tool. (Cardinal's agreement with hospitals prohibits them from revealing data tied to individual institutions other than the provider's own; manufacturers have access only to aggregate data.)

Cardinal Information Corporation's (CIC) strategy is to develop self-sustaining profitable businesses that throw off data that would be useful in other parts of the pharmaceutical food chain. Another of CIC's information products is Scriptline™, designed to help independent pharmacies receive the maximum allowable insurance reimbursement on covered prescriptions. (Frequent pharmaceutical price in-creases can result in lower-than-allowable claims by pharmacies. Further, reimbursement policies vary by class of drug—generic versus proprietary—and by carrier, creating an information management bur-den for pharmacies.)

In summary, Cardinal Health has not been content to use data warehousing to solve data integration and decision support problems. The company is aggressively mining its data resources for opportunities that will result in new revenue. Data warehousing technology plays a key role in this data mining strategy.

Key Success Factors

Take Advantage of the Different Uses of Data Warehousing

Data warehousing has a variety of uses both for Cardinal and its cus-tomers. Data warehousing has been used to help integrate the data and business processes of a company that grew rapidly through acquisition, to provide internal and external decision support, and to provide Cardi-nal with new information business opportunities.

The different uses of data warehousing provide different kinds of benefits. Properly deployed, data warehousing can enable cross-unit co-ordination and management reporting, reduce operating costs, and in-crease revenues. Valid rationales for data warehousing projects can be based on both technical and business concerns.

Make Organizational Changes Where Needed

Many benefits of data warehousing require organization change, such as reduced local autonomy or increased performance measurement and control.

Ensure Data Quality

Warehoused data will be used only if people trust their accuracy. Rec-onciliation to demonstrate data quality may be necessary to promote use of the data warehouse. Technology is not the major barrier to data quality and reporting accuracy. There are many business and cultural barriers that cannot be addressed solely by technical means.

Move Quickly

Business does not stand still for the perfect data warehouse design. Effective adopters solve short-term business and technical problems linked to long-term business and technical goals, then improve these short-term solutions over time.

Provide Support Above and Beyond Training

Training is necessary but not sufficient to overcome people's reluctance to do hands-on report access and analysis.

Make Good Use of External Data

Effective decision support via data warehousing makes good use of external data resources.

Data Mining Requires Special Efforts

Effective mining of data resources may require special initiatives. Many pressing short-term issues distract attention from strategic use of corporate data resources.

People Interviewed

Dave Blickensderfer, Manager, Software Development, Customer Information Systems

Phillip A. Greth, Executive Vice President and Chief Information Officer

Gina Harrobin, Manager, Decision Support Systems, Customer Information Systems

Fritz Kerieger, Vice President/General Manager, Cardinal Information Corporation

Don Lyle, Director, Customer Support Services National Accounts

Tracy Maloney, Manager, Marketing Projects

Richard J. Miller, Corporate Vice President, Controller

Ronald E. Morgan, Senior Vice President, Information Systems, Cardinal Distribution

Michael Proulx, Vice President, Operations

R. Scott Summers, Manager, Customer Systems Marketing, Customer Information Systems

Print Sources

Cardinal Health Information Technology Overview and Strategic Plan. Company internal document, no date.

Levin, Stephen. Outcomes: Changing Drug Distribution's Cardinal Rule. *In Vivo The Business & Medicine Report.* Vol. 16, no. 6 (June 1988): 1–8.

Rockart, John F., and Michael E. Treacy. CEO Goes On-Line. *Harvard Business Review.* Vol. 60, no. 1 (January-February 1982): 82–88.

8

Lessons Learned

The literature on data warehousing strongly suggests that *the* reason for companies to undertake data warehousing is to acquire the capability of data mining. By contrast, our interviews and cases suggest that relatively few companies are currently mining their internal and external data sources. On the other hand, quite a few companies have undertaken data warehousing for purposes other than data mining, and they are achieving benefits from these nondata mining uses.

Put differently, the term "data mining" is too narrow to convey the reasons companies undertake data warehousing and the benefits they achieve from it. Companies can benefit from data warehousing as a solution to inefficiencies in the production and distribution of routine management reports; they can also benefit from data warehousing as an engine for new data products to be offered to customers. At the same time, the more familiar term "decision support" is too non-specific to capture the whys and wherefores of data warehousing. We found four distinct patterns of using data warehouses in our cases, which we call management reporting/decision support, systems and organizational integration, data mining, and new data products. Briefly, these uses are as follows:

- *Management reporting/decision support.* This use of data warehousing is intended to facilitate the production and distribution of routine management reports and/or ad hoc model-based analyses. The reports and analyses may be distributed on paper or electronically (via e-mail or intranet). Many of the reports generated in this use of data warehousing were previously produced in the organization using other technologies (e.g., mainframe-based query and reporting tools for operational databases; PC-based spreadsheet programs) and/or multiple-source systems. Most of what falls under this heading is simple summarization, comparison with prior periods, trend analysis, and exception reporting.

Occasionally, more sophisticated ad hoc modeling and statistical analysis is done. But this use of data warehousing does not approximate data mining or knowledge discovery, which is generally characterized by inductive methods and techniques such as artificial intelligence or neural networking. (Neural networks learn through pattern matching and the equivalent of behavioral reinforcement.) Rather, it is closer to what used to be called management control, exception reporting, or even EIS. All[1] our case-study sites used data warehousing in this way. (See table 8.1.)

- *Systems and organizational integration.* This use of data warehousing can be understood as a substitute for, or transition to, other types of integration of data, transaction processing systems, or business processes. Because of the way organizational information processing systems have historically developed, most organizations of any size or age are currently experiencing problems owing to lack of integration in their core transaction processing systems. Some have addressed lack of integration problems by redeveloping their systems, perhaps using middleware and/or the object-oriented programming paradigm. (This solution seems most common in the financial services industry.) Others have addressed integration needs by using enterprise software systems. (Consider Microsoft's use of SAP R/3 to replace numerous unintegrated financial systems.) Still others find that neither of these solutions meet their integration needs, at least in the short run. For these organizations, data warehousing can be a substitute for change in core operational systems or a transitional integration step while change in the core operational systems is under way. Three of our case-study sites used data warehousing, as opposed to enterprise resource planning (ERP), as a primary integration strategy.

- *Data mining.* A third use of data warehousing we observed is the classic "knowledge discovery" use of data mining. A pioneering example is Frito-Lay's use of data warehousing technology to "discover" successful patterns of brand promotion.[2] Among our cases, this use was most clearly observed at BankAmerica, another data warehousing pioneer. Most data mining applications are developed for internal use. Value is derived from better decisions about the allocation of resources, the prevention of waste or fraud or quality problems, and so on.

■ *New data products.* Cardinal Health used data warehousing to deliver to external customers new data products developed from the organization's in-house and purchased information assets. Value is derived from revenues from the sale of the new product/service. (Or, in the case of a public service offering, such as Envirofacts, value is derived from improved customer service.[3]) We had found no direct mention of this use of data warehousing in the literature, although there is increasing attention to the strategic reuse of data and the development of data products for sale to customers outside the organization.[4]

Table 8.1 shows how these uses of data warehousing were distributed across six cases, including the four we conducted for this report and the two we conducted earlier (Bashein, et al. 1997). Table 8.1 combines data mining and new data products. The table shows that data warehousing is almost always used to serve routine and ad hoc management reporting needs of the organizations that adopt it. Integration needs, however, can be met in different ways: Two (Microsoft and ALARIS) of five organizations for which we have data about integration used enterprise software, such as that sold by SAP AG, as a primary strategy for handling integration needs. Three (Kraft, MSC.Software,

Table 8.1
Data Warehousing Uses That Were Studied in Six Cases

Company	Reporting Needs	Integration Needs	Mining or New Data Products
Microsoft	data warehouse	ERP	
ALARIS	data warehouse	ERP	
Kraft	data warehouse	data warehouse	
MSC.Software	data warehouse	data warehouse	
Cardinal Health	data warehouse	data warehouse	data warehouse
BankAmerica	not studied	not studied	data warehouse

and Cardinal Health) used data warehousing to enable some measure of integration, in conjunction with redevelopment of core transaction processing systems. Only in Cardinal Health and BankAmerica did we see any appreciable use of data warehousing for internal data mining or for delivering new data products to customers.

In other words, for the companies we studied, data warehousing is not a single, monolithic technology. Instead, it is four different *uses* of technology. This observation is important because the benefits a company achieves from using a technology like data warehousing depend in part on what the company sets out to achieve. Further, different goals suggest different plans of action. The best way to use data warehousing for better management reporting may differ substantially from the best way to use it for integration or for data mining. Therefore, the wise organization will apply lessons learned from companies with similar, rather than dissimilar, data warehousing goals.

In the next sections of this chapter, we discuss our findings specific to each of the four uses of data warehousing technology. For each use, we discuss the need the technology can be used to fill and some of the issues we observed in how the technology is effectively or ineffectively deployed for that use.

Data Warehousing for Management Reporting/Decision Support

One important need for data warehousing—common to most companies—is to provide a good technological environment for management reporting and decision support.

Needs Satisfied by the Technology

Data warehousing provides a consistent technology platform for consolidating data and performing management reporting. Writing reports against a data warehouse can be much simpler, less error prone, and less costly in terms of maintenance effort than attempting to make complex queries against an operational database on an ongoing basis. OLAP, a core component of data warehousing, is a superior technology for deriving (by summarizing, eliminating, restating, modeling, etc.)

information from the data in corporate transaction processing systems. Combined with other components of a data warehousing solution, it lessens the tradeoffs between power and ease of use that have plagued mainframe and PC-based decision support tools.

All companies need routine management reporting and ad hoc analysis, regardless of the level of integration in their core transaction processing systems. Consider the experience of many companies that have recently adopted integrated enterprise systems, such as those offered by Baan, SAP, Oracle, Peoplesoft, and JD Edwards. For the most part, larger and more structurally complex organizations have not been satisfied with the reporting capabilities enterprise software packages provide. Built-in reporting capabilities have not been flexible enough to meet the reporting requirements of multidivisional, multiproduct firms operating in multiple locations. Even companies that find the built-in reporting structures adequate may be dissatisfied with the extent to which built-in reporting tools slow the performance of operational systems. Therefore, even companies that have completely integrated their operational systems by means of enterprise software may still need an alternative solution for decision support needs. Many companies are currently meeting those needs by acquiring additional reporting software and/or adopting data warehousing technology (either from the enterprise system vendor or from some other source).

The two ERP-using companies in our set of six cases, Microsoft and ALARIS, are no exceptions to this rule. Microsoft quickly determined that SAP's reporting tool would not work for casual (versus expert) users of financial reports. Therefore, Microsoft used data warehousing, easy-to-use query/reporting tools, and the intranet to support its goals for on-demand, do-it-yourself financial publishing. Similarly, when we visited ALARIS, it was searching for a better solution to its management reporting needs—needs the company had determined could not be met solely by SAP's built-in reporting. ALARIS expected that a data warehouse for SAP data would be the solution to its management reporting needs.

Kraft, MSC.Software, and Cardinal Health all had pressing business problems that demanded better solutions for routine management reporting. For MSC.Software, the problem involved reporting and forecasting revenues from multiyear software leases. Kraft and Cardinal Health needed to be able to tell their customers how much in total the customers were buying. With their nonintegrated sales and inventory tracking systems, these companies could not answer their customers' questions.

In general, the problem of routine and ad hoc management reporting can be summarized as follows:

- *Core transaction processing systems are not optimized for reporting.* Regardless of how well integrated they are, the core transaction processing systems of organizations are not designed to support reporting; they are designed to support transaction processing. Running queries and reports against operational databases decreases the performance of operational systems, slowing response times for people working in customer-focused business processes like sales order entry.

- *Reporting often involves data from multiple sources.* Even when a company's core transaction systems are integrated, managers often need to answer questions that require data from multiple sources (e.g., historical data not maintained in the transaction system) and/or external data. Without a solution like data warehousing, the production of routine and ad hoc management reports can require manual integration efforts, such as ad hoc program writing by IS staff or manually rekeying data from paper reports into spreadsheets. Financial specialists at Kraft Foods described how they had to analyze T&E information requests after the shared services organization was formed but before integrated systems were built to support the new business process: Analysts had to go through stacks of expense reports manually to add up the number of trips to particular locations.

- *Management reporting often entails huge hidden costs.* Some of the hidden costs of management reporting were known well before the days of data warehousing. Management reports are often created to solve temporary business needs. But when the needs change (or new management comes in), old reports often continue to be produced, with attendant waste. (Veteran IS managers describe efforts to combat this problem: "If you want to continue getting this report, please fill in this form and mail it back.")

Fragmented systems and hard-to-use data access and reporting tools have led to a situation in which most organizations have chauffeurs to produce special reports. Sometimes, the chauffeurs are IS professionals working in information centers. IS specialists at MSC.Software and Cardinal Health told us that the demands on them to produce special reports were so great that they had no time to improve the systems environment.

In other cases, the chauffeurs are functional specialists, such as the engineering analysts at ALARIS, the financial analysts at Microsoft, and the marketing and sales analysts at Cardinal Health. Even more invidious than the excessive use of specialist human resources, a bad reporting environment can result in inappropriate organizational conflict. Several of the people we interviewed explained that the goal of data warehousing in their companies was to produce "one answer for the company, so that instead of fighting about the data, we can fight about what we should do about it." A good management reporting environment can substantially reduce conflict over which data sources, data definitions, and analytic models to use, allowing the company to focus on the interpretation of data and appropriate business responses.

Issues Raised by Data Warehousing for Management Reporting/Decision Support

As we look at how the companies in our study were using data warehousing for management reporting/decision support, it is clear that companies planning to adopt this use of data warehousing technology face several challenges, including the following:

- *Unclear justification of need.* The hidden costs of management reporting in most organizations are, well, hidden. When executives request reports analyzing various business situations, they usually get them, and they usually get them fast. They do not see the difficulties their assistants face in producing these documents: begging programmers to write reports, manually culling data, and rekeying data from various reports. Consequently, executives may not be receptive to multimillion dollar requests to implement data warehouses to solve the organization's reporting problems.

■ *Intended users.* The intended users of management reporting/decision support environments can be anyone in the organization: IS specialists, business executives, and analysts. The intended users can range in skill from output-only use, to simple analysis, to "power use" or highly sophisticated analysis. Organizations planning to adopt data warehousing must make a choice: Do they intend to provide support for people who are doing analysis and reporting work today (e.g., the analysts at ALARIS)? Or do they intend to expand access to, and use of, analysis and reporting tools to any authorized person in the organization on a do-it-yourself basis (e.g., Microsoft)? The answers to these questions hold important implications. "Everyone as user" requires much easier-to-use data access and analysis tools than "data warehousing in support of expert analysts." At Kraft, the decision was made to use Business Objects as a query tool for financial analysts, since that tool was built around Excel, a program with which most financial analysts are very familiar. Organizations planning to expand use of decision analysis tools to new users may need to plan for more training in the structure of the data, analysis techniques, and interpretation. In addition, they may need to pay greater attention to issues of data security.[5] On the other hand, the rewards of this strategy may be improved organizational decisionmaking and learning.

■ *Distribution method.* The desire to expand data access to new user populations usually inspires companies to consider new distribution approaches, such as replacing paper financial statements with print-on-demand reports via the intranet at Microsoft. However, interviewees in several companies told us that many users are not yet ready for substantial changes in management reporting, whether the changes affected the *medium* of distribution or a shift in *timing*, from periodic snapshot reporting to continuous process monitoring. For example, IS specialists at one company told us that, for some sales executives, "it's not a report unless it's printed on paper." For a counterexample, planners at Frito-Lay, Inc., used data warehousing capabilities to increase the number of yearly planning cycles from two to three, with a commensurate increase in profit-taking opportunities.[6] In general, companies that viewed functional analysts as the intended user of data warehousing reporting capabilities were less aggressive than other companies in considering changes to the medium and timing of managerial reporting.

Data Warehousing for Systems and Organizational Integration

A second important use of data warehousing—used as a primary integration strategy by three of the companies we studied—is to provide some measure of integration of data, systems, and business processes without (or in conjunction with) changes in core transaction processing systems.

Needs Satisfied by the Technology

Many organizations are currently burdened with legacy IS environments. Because of technical constraints when many core transaction processing systems were built (as many as 20 years ago), larger organizations have found themselves saddled with unintegrated systems, redundant and inconsistent data stores, and software maintenance headaches. Other organizations (including Kraft and Cardinal Health) have found themselves in the same position because they grew by acquisition of independent companies with their own information systems, which were not replaced with corporate systems when the companies were acquired. Lack of integrated data, systems, or business processes means that a complex organization cannot easily act as one entity in relations with customers and cannot effectively make corporate decisions, such as negotiating corporate purchasing agreements with suppliers. Lack of systems integration and software inflexibility also prevents the kind of business process reengineering that many companies view as essential to future competitiveness.

The situation has become sufficiently galling that it, coupled with last year's Y2K scare, helped fuel the boom in enterprise systems software sales. But some organizations have decided for various reasons that enterprise systems are not right for them. Organizations that are basically satisfied with their software functionality and only want to improve software integration and the user interface often choose to reengineer their own custom software rather than go to the expense of adopting ERP. Second, the organizations in some industries, such as financial and other kinds of services, have not always been well served by ERP software functionality. Third, some organizations view the adoption of ERP as inappropriate for organizational reasons.

Among the companies we studied, three organizations with needs for data, systems, and business integration chose to pursue those needs with data warehousing, rather than with ERP. MSC.Software had originally viewed enterprise software as the solution to its revenue accounting problems. Later, however, it found out that its enterprise software vendor did not have revenue accounting software for leasing businesses and was not likely to produce it. Similarly, existing enterprise systems did not have the functionality to replace Cardinal Health's custom-developed distribution systems. Kraft explicitly considered ERP but rejected that solution as politically infeasible in light of Kraft's long tradition of decentralization and functionally driven decisionmaking.

Data warehousing has two additional benefits as a (partial) solution to organizational lack-of-integration problems. First, data warehousing can enable some organizations to make business changes while avoiding the need to make systems changes. MSC.Software provides a good example. Because MSC.Software's products are leased, they provide revenues and commission income over multiple years. But sales reps turn over, and sales territories are periodically restructured to respond to various business situations. Absent data warehousing technology, keeping track of the revenue and commission impacts of changes in sales territories would require difficult and expensive changes in MSC.Software's core transaction systems. Today, MSC.Software is able to reorganize the way it does business with minimal systems impact—the company simply rebuilds its revenue accounting data warehouse to reflect new assumptions about the sales territories and customer assignments to sales reps.

A second benefit of data warehousing used for integration purposes is that the technology can ease the transition to enterprise systems or other types of core systems integration. For example, organizations that must keep many years of product or customer history data generally will not want to load the history data into their new enterprise systems, because the processing and storage requirements will be very expensive. Instead, they can load only current data into the new ERP systems but maintain access to historical data and the ability to combine historical and current data through a data warehouse. ALARIS maintained historical data in its data warehouse during and after the transition to the new SAP system. This strategy can also work when the integration solution does not involve ERP. For example, Cardinal Health consolidated 11 distribution systems into two and eventually to one by building its corporate warehouses of sales and customer data.

Issues Raised by Data Warehousing for Systems and Organizational Integration

As we look at how the companies in our study were using data warehousing for systems and organizational integration, it is clear that companies planning to adopt this use of data warehousing technology face several challenging issues. Among them are the following:

■ *Changes in data collection systems.* Ultimately, organizations are limited in their use of data warehousing to the data they have already collected (or acquired from third parties). If needed data do not exist in the base systems, data warehousing is not going to create the data. Changes in the core transaction processing systems may still be needed to satisfy organizations' data integration needs. For example, interviewees at Kraft Foods explained that they did not have transaction-level integration between their sales systems and their financial systems. Consequently, they could not trace a particular sale directly through to its top- and bottom-line impacts, as some companies that adopt ERP systems can. Another consumer products company we interviewed explained that its data warehousing efforts began with a complete redesign of core transaction processing systems to collect data at a much finer level of detail than previously: That company can now make promotion decisions at the level of an individual store rather than at the level of an account or sales territory.

■ *Political and human challenges.* The difficulty of change management involved in using data warehousing for systems and organizational integration is the same in form and intensity as that involved in consolidating or integrating core transaction processing systems (and hence, ERP implementation). Managers and process workers still need to be convinced of the value of commonality and data sharing. They have the same concerns about the new visibility (e.g., into individual or business unit performance) brought about by data warehousing technology. The more the data warehouse is seen as an enterprisewide solution, as opposed to a particular subject-oriented solution, the greater the likelihood of political issues during project justification and construction of the data warehouse.

■ *Gaining consensus on data naming, definitions, modeling.* When data warehousing is used for systems and organizational integration, the organization will almost certainly need to standardize and consolidate definitions of various data elements. At Kraft Foods, for example, the old General Foods divisions had done things very differently from the old Kraft divisions. Building data warehouses and moving toward systems consolidation required carefully working the political consensus among various factions. Sometimes, it is not necessary to achieve complete consensus, or conversely, to arrive at a decision by fiat. One interviewee explained:

> It used to drive me crazy trying to push for consensus on defining every single element in the data warehouse. Finally, it dawned on me that this was not really necessary. Now, sometimes when consensus is hard to obtain, I permit the definition of two different data elements instead of one. I might call one of them "sales inventory" and another "production inventory." As for which of these two definitions will wind up being more useful [for managerial decisionmaking] over time, that's an empirical question. Maybe eventually, one of these data elements will have less predictive power than the other. If so, I'd expect it to fall into disuse. But in the meantime, it might be better for organizational learning to have competing definitions: It might help foster a scientific approach to management decisionmaking in this company.

■ *Importance of data quality.* If people are to give up systems and data sources with which they are comfortable and accept a single, enterprisewide data source instead, they must be absolutely convinced that the quality of the data in the warehouse matches that of their trusted data sources. They are not likely to take corporate's word about data quality; data quality must be *proved*. One of the strongest conclusions we took from our fieldwork is that concerns about data quality can break a data warehousing effort. Therefore, it is necessary, for political and technical reasons, that data warehouse developers conduct a public proof of data quality.

At Cardinal Health, this proof consisted of reconciling the CSD with the general ledger. The reconciliation showed that there was indeed cause for concern: The two data sources were initially millions of dollars apart. But even when developers know the data to be accurate, potential users need to be convinced. That's why one of the systems specialists at Kraft Foods took such pains to show her users that reports from the old and the new systems matched to the very penny. It should be reiterated that the time and cost associated with the data part of a data warehousing project can be huge—some experts say as much as 70 percent of the project total. But, if this part of the project is not done well, the consequences for user acceptance are likely to be negative.

■ *Importance of training in data structures.* In every case-study site, interviewees emphasized the need for people to understand the structure and definitions of data in the warehouse. Training and qualification (via testing) of data warehouse users are commonly discussed as essential strategies for preventing erroneous analyses. Such training can have the added advantage of fostering a "one company" view of the business.

Data Warehousing for Data Mining and New Data Products

Data mining—the sophisticated secondary analysis of warehoused data for purposes of discovering potential new relationships—is widely viewed as the primary reason for organizations to do data warehousing. (Data warehousing is a prerequisite for mining.) We found that, however beneficial it might be, relatively few organizations were doing data mining. Conversely, however, we also found a new mining-like use of data warehousing—as an engine for delivering the capabilities of new data products to customers.

Needs Satisfied by the Technology

Many companies can say, as Cardinal Health did, "We have a tremendous amount of data that we're not doing much with. How can we best make use of our information resources?" Answering this question is the goal of the research field of knowledge discovery. The concerns of knowledge discovery extend well beyond the simple routine and ad hoc management exception reporting discussed earlier. Through the use of sophisticated statistical and nonstatistical decision modeling, knowledge discovery specialists aim to bring power and discipline to the art of managerial decisionmaking. Among the specific nonroutine uses of data warehousing for knowledge discovery are detecting fraud in the insurance and telecommunications industries, identifying profitable customers and potential customers, identifying threats to customer retention, analyzing product quality problems, and identifying new product and service opportunities.

We think that most companies can benefit from data mining. However, many companies lack the perceived need or motivation to do data mining. These companies may be satisfied with their existing managerial decisionmaking, perhaps unaware of the benefits to be gained from data mining, or all too aware of the improvements they can still make with existing management decision analysis tools (i.e., the management reporting and ad hoc analysis uses of data warehousing discussed earlier).

In some cases, organizations (unlike BankAmerica) that do not deliberately set out to do data mining may come to embrace it after developing a data warehouse for other reasons. For example, Nabisco apparently did not intend to get hard-dollar business benefits from its data warehouse. Its goals were more modest and technical: to get sales and accounting transaction data off its mainframe computers and make the data easily available for use by sales executives and financial analysts. Almost immediately, however, the company discovered that it could use the data warehouse to identify product profits and losses and potential cost savings across its more than 8,000 products. For example, the company was able to eliminate some unprofitable holiday packs during the Christmas season.[7]

Naturally, Nabisco will now be on the lookout for additional data mining opportunities. Generally, however, it is not a good idea to build a data warehouse in hopes that it might eventually lead to data mining uses and benefits. On the other hand, if a clear business case justifies the data warehouse for reporting and/or integration purposes, future data mining use might provide huge unexpected benefits.

The literature on data warehousing does not discuss the additional use that we observed at Cardinal Health—data warehousing as an engine for delivering new data products and services to *customers*. Here, the value to the developer derives from the revenues generated by the new product or service. Cardinal Health has not yet used data warehousing extensively for data mining in the traditional sense, although interviewees there expected such use in the future. In the traditional sense, data mining means finding or proving new relationships in company data with important implications for how the company does business (e.g., targeting marketing initiatives at individuals with certain characteristics or investigating certain situations for possible fraud). Instead, Cardinal Health mined its data assets for new data products and services that it could sell to its customers and suppliers—hospitals, pharmacies, and drug manufacturers. The development of new data products and services is viewed as an important strategic opportunity for many businesses, even those that mainly produce tangible goods and services.[8] However, this activity has not usually been associated with the technology of data warehousing. We found that data warehousing can be used as an engine for delivering products to customers, as in the case of Cardinal Health's Jericho.

Issues Raised by Data Warehousing for
Data Mining and New Data Products

As we look at how the companies in our study were using data warehousing for data mining and delivering new data products and services, it is clear that companies planning to adopt this use of data warehousing technology face several challenging issues. Among them are the following:

■ *Identifying intended users.* As with the management reporting/decision support use of data warehousing, the intended user (any authorized person versus a specialist analyst) is an important issue for data mining and new data products. The intended user should determine both the type of access and analysis tools used and the levels of training, support, and security provided. Generally speaking, data mining is more likely than management reporting/decision support to require "power users," who are thoroughly versed in both data structures and data analysis techniques (to avoid the problem of spurious results, see below). Further, some interviewees pointed out that knowledge discovery requires a very different set of analytic skills than the hypothesis testing routines commonly taught in business schools. Consequently, successful data miners may have to develop their own training programs.

■ *Safeguarding privacy.* Data mining and new data products generally entail secondary analysis of corporate and/or purchasing data, often about customers or potential customers. Use of customer data for reasons other than those for which they were originally collected raises issues of privacy. In Europe, stringent legislation prevents most secondary uses of customer data. Because of the potential for public backlash, experts advise U.S. companies to develop and enforce policies designed to protect customers' data privacy.

■ *Avoiding spurious results.* Data mining offers the promise of exciting new discoveries that will bring large payoffs, such as the often-cited diapers-and-beer relationship. On the other hand, companies could potentially lose big by betting on unproven results. Experts advise companies to adopt rigorous measures to test relationships discovered in data mining, and they also recommend controlled pilot tests of marketing and other programs designed on the basis of knowledge discovery. And, as emphasized above, they also advise extensive training in data structures and definitions, not just analysis tools.

■ *Avoiding incorrect conclusions.* One danger of data mining is the possibility of incorrect conclusions drawn by people who have easy access to data and analysis tools but limited understanding of the data structures and analytical techniques. Potential solutions include limiting access to highly trained analysts or instituting a mentoring program, as was done at BankAmerica.

■ *Finding appropriate external data sources and business models.* Data mining and new data products are more likely than management reporting/decision support to require external data. Identifying and vetting external data sources is key to the success of these uses of data warehousing, as the case of Cardinal Health shows. In addition, when data warehousing is used as an engine of a new data product to be sold to customers, organizations need an appropriate business model for the new enterprise. At Cardinal Health, for instance, developers of the Jericho™ product were anxious to add value to acquired external data: Merely purchasing data for resale was not viewed as a sustainable business model for Cardinal. Also, early on, Cardinal decided that products like Jericho warranted their own business unit rather than having to compete for time and attention in a unit established to pursue other business opportunities.

Summary

Our findings from the cases and other interviews suggest that data warehousing is not *one* technology, but at least four different *uses* of technology. Organizations adopt data warehousing for very different reasons, they go about using it in very different ways, and they gain different kinds of benefits from the different uses. Four uses we observed were data warehousing for management reporting/decision support, data warehousing for systems and organizational integration, data warehousing for data mining, and data warehousing for delivering new data products or services to customers. No one of these uses is inherently superior. Each can provide benefits in particular circumstances. But each use raises different issues and the possibility of different best practices. Wise companies are well advised to benchmark their data warehousing approach against that of companies with similar circumstances and goals.

Endnotes

1. We do not have relevant data for BankAmerica, but it is plausible to assume that the company also uses data warehousing this way.

2. "Frito-Lay, Inc.: A Strategic Transition—1987-92 (Abridged)." *Harvard Business School* 9-195-238 (1997).

3. www.epa.gov/

4. Marc. H. Meyer and Michael H. Zack. "The Design and Development of Information Products." *Sloan Management Review,* Vol. 37, no. 3 (Spring 1996): 43–59.

5. Bashein, Barbara J., M. Lynne Markus, and Jane B. Finley. *Safety Nets: Secrets of Effective Information Technology Controls.* Morristown, NJ: Financial Executives Research Foundation, Inc. (1997).

6. Bashein, et al. *Safety Nets* (1997).

7. "Frito-Lay, Inc." (1997).

8. Blaise Zerenga. "Nabisco Ekes Surprise Savings Out of OLAP Data Marts: Fine-Toothed Analysis of Product Lines Helps the Snack Food Giant Improve Efficiency and Cut Costs." *Infoworld* (September 21, 1998): 78.

9. Meyer and Zack. (1996).

9

Recommendations

This chapter includes some specific recommendations that executives and managers who are building or planning data warehouses can apply. Data warehousing technologies can provide relatively big paybacks to small and medium-sized companies. However, a word of caution is in order. Data warehousing recommendations are not one size fits all. Recommendations vary according to the organization's size, industry and competitive environment, financial and human resources, IT sophistication, culture, legacy systems environment, and so on.

With this caveat in mind, we have assembled some general recommendations, presented as tables, in several categories:

- ■ *Reasons for building a data warehouse*—Key questions and considerations are included as they relate to four uses of data warehousing technologies: (1) management reporting/decision support, (2) systems and organizational integration, (3) data mining, and (4) new data products.

- ■ *Approaches to building a data warehouse*—Pros, cons, and recommendations are summarized for the three categories of approaches to building a data warehouse: (1) enterprise solution, (2) evolutionary approach, and (3) package approach.

- ■ *Technology, data, and organizational checklists*—Key questions and considerations are summarized.

These general recommendations are based on our analysis and synthesis across all segments of the study—literature review, vendor reviews, company survey, and case studies. The questions are stated so that a "yes" or "does not apply" answer is desirable. A "no" answer flags an area of potential concern.

More specific recommendations that better fit particular circumstances and situations can be gleaned from rereading the individual case studies (ALARIS Medical Systems, BankAmerica,[1] Cardinal

Health, Kraft Foods, MSC.Software, and Microsoft[2]) and chapters 3 and 8.

One overarching recommendation relates to the business problems that set the stage for a data warehouse development project. Data warehouse initiatives are prone to becoming never-ending analysis/paralysis projects. Relating the warehouse to a pressing business problem and satisfying a pressing business need are the most effective ways to manage this risk. Business conditions do not stand still and wait for the perfect data warehouse design. Therefore, effective adopters of data warehouse solutions need to solve short-term business and technical problems linked to long-term business and technical goals. Then they can evolve and improve their short-term data warehousing solutions over time.

Table 9.1
Reasons for Building a Data Warehouse

Uses	Key Questions	Considerations
Management reporting/decision support—This use is intended to facilitate the production and distribution of routine management reports and/or ad-hoc, model-based analyses.	1. Does your organization have a pressing business need that can be addressed successfully by a data warehouse? 2. Can you articulate the business need in a couple of sentences? 3. Have you identified the sources (internal and external) of data for populating your warehouse? 4. Have you evaluated the extraction, cleaning, and conversion requirements for each data source? 5. Have you identified all potential users of a warehouse and assessed their needs in terms of query types and support services?	▪ If your organization has little or no experience with data warehousing, a management-reporting warehouse is a good place to begin. ▪ Requirements for routine or ad hoc management reports not currently available can present a pressing business need—a favorable environment for a data warehouse project. ▪ Data warehouses can simplify the creation and maintenance of routine reports.

Table 9.1
Reasons for Building a Data Warehouse

Uses	Key Questions	Considerations
Management reporting/ decision support—This use is intended to facilitate the production and distribution of routine management reports and/or ad-hoc, model-based analyses.	6. Will both data and tool training be provided?	■ Data may need to come from multiple sources (internal and/or external). The volume of available information surpasses organizations' abilities to absorb and use it.
		■ Warehouse users may need chauffeur-driven services or do-it-yourself support. The do-it-yourself users may need point-and-click menus or sophisticated query tools.
		■ The low-risk approach is to start users with point-and-click menus and transition to more sophisticated queries.
		■ Self-service reporting tools make data available to a wider audience and can provide relatively quick paybacks.
		■ Organizations typically underestimate the importance and challenge of learning the data (definitions and structures).
		■ Training classes focus for the most part on using the query and reporting tools, when they should also address the data and the interpretation of analysis results.
		■ Individuals with insufficient understanding of the data and the business may draw improper conclusions.

(Continued)

Table 9.1
Reasons for Building a Data Warehouse

(Continued)

Uses	Key Questions	Considerations
Systems and organizational integration—Data warehousing can be a substitute for or a transition to other types of information systems and/or business unit structures. A data warehouse can be a substitute for changes in core operational systems or a transitional integration step while changes in the core operational systems are under way.	1. Does your organization have systems and/or data resources that need to be integrated? 2. Is this an inopportune time for your organization to redevelop existing systems or to adopt enterprise solutions? (If so, data warehousing may be a good short-term approach to improving systems and/or data integration.)	■ This is a good place for many organizations to start with their data warehousing initiatives. ■ Organizations can make effective progress toward systems consolidation and integration with data warehousing. ■ Organizations can use a data warehouse for merging data from disparate, legacy systems: consolidating information from distributed worldwide operations, integrating new data resulting from mergers and acquisitions, combining actual and forecasted data, or integrating supplemental external data. ■ One of the frequently overlooked benefits of data warehousing is that it can serve as a repository for historical data, limiting the burden on new ERP systems.

129

Table 9.1
Reasons for Building a Data Warehouse

Uses	Key Questions	Considerations
Data mining—This use of data warehousing implies knowledge discovery. Value is derived from better decisions about the allocation of resources (e.g., advertising budgets or new customer solicitations), the prevention of waste, fraud, or quality problems, etc.	1. Does your organization have a culture of measuring and rewarding performance? 2. Do you have reason to believe that improved decisionmaking would lead to significant financial gains? 3. Are knowledge workers in the affected areas of the business open to a scientific (as opposed to an intuitive) approach to making important organizational decisions? 4. Does your organization have adequate internal controls and security measures in place to ensure privacy?	▪ This use of data warehousing is generally not for beginners. ▪ Training analysts to do discovery is more difficult than training for hypothesis testing. ▪ Effective data mining usually requires external as well as internal data resources. ▪ Effective data mining may require special initiatives. Many pressing short-term issues distract attention from the strategic use of corporate data resources. ▪ Safeguards against spurious results must be adopted. ▪ Individuals with insufficient understanding of the data, the tools, and the business may draw improper conclusions.

(Continued)

Table 9.1
Reasons for Building a Data Warehouse

(Continued)

Uses	Key Questions	Considerations
New data products— A data warehouse comprised of internal and external (purchased) data can be used to provide and deliver new data products to external customers. This is a relatively new use of data warehousing.	1. Do you consider your organization to be rich in data resources that would be of benefit to some other parties? 2. Have you carefully analyzed all legal and data privacy issues? 3. Have you conducted focus groups or other market research with potential users of new data products? 4. Have you considered the ongoing infrastructure and support requirements for new data products? 5. Have you clearly stated the business model for each new data product (e.g., pricing, marketing, operations, etc.)?	▪ Data privacy must be managed carefully. ▪ Developing new data products may require the purchase of external data resources. ▪ Investments in new data products may be slow to provide any paybacks.

Table 9.2
Approaches to Building a Data Warehouse

Approach and Description	Pros	Cons	Recommendations
Enterprise solution— The data warehouse is an enterprise-wide repository of key organizational data.	■ Many experts believe that this approach results in the best design. ■ This approach mandates a comprehensive data planning effort. ■ This approach promotes extensive data cleaning and restructuring. ■ Specialized department or business unit data marts can be developed from the main enterprise-wide warehouse.	■ This approach can take too long, and cost too much—the "ready, aim, aim, aim, fire" approach. ■ Enterprise solutions are particularly difficult for companies with worldwide operations and/or acquisitions. ■ Organizations find it difficult to obtain consensus on key data elements and their definitions. ■ It may be impossible to design a grand architecture that works well for all parts of the business.	■ Consider an evolutionary or package approach to gain experience before undertaking an enterprise solution. ■ Carefully select participants for the data-design team, and ensure their full-time participation. Every business unit should be represented on the data-design team. Team members should have: 1) a good understanding of their business unit's data requirements, 2) authority to make decisions on key data elements and their definitions, and 3) good interpersonal skills in order to reach consensus. ■ Establish a firm timetable for the data design effort, and adhere to it.

Table 9.2
Approaches to Building a Data Warehouse

Approach and Description	Pros	Cons	Recommendations
Evolutionary approach— The pragmatic approach of building data marts to deal with specific business needs.	■ This popular approach engenders enthusiasm and support from the business units and the IS development staff. ■ An organization can get a working prototype up and running quickly—the "aim, fire, reaim, refire" approach. ■ Significant benefits can be obtained from quick and dirty data warehouse implementations.	■ Organizations adopting the evolutionary approach can wind up with a proliferation of data marts with different standards, technologies, and data definitions—a nightmare for service and support. ■ Many evolutionary warehouses require costly retrofitting work to improve performance and/or data quality.	■ Develop a flexible, overall architecture with an eye toward eventually building a corporate data warehouse from individual data marts. ■ Use the architecture to guide the development of the individual data marts. ■ Establish requirements assessment as an iterative process. ■ Let the warehouse evolve.

(Continued)

Table 9.2
Approaches to Building a Data Warehouse

Approach and Description	Pros	Cons	Recommendations
Package approach—There are two types of data warehouse packages: 1. Packages that integrate with ERP systems. ERP vendors provide these packages to work with their operational databases and data structures. 2. Packages that are designed for a particular industry or business problem (e.g., customer prospecting). Systems consulting firms provide these packages and may include preloaded external data and preformatted queries and analyses.	■ Adopting the package approach avoids the need to integrate ERP and data warehouse technologies from different vendors. ■ The package approach avoids reinventing the wheel around common business problems. ■ Packages capitalize on lessons learned from experienced designers.	■ The package approach is emerging; there is little experience to date with data warehouse packages. ■ The one-size-fits-all design may not satisfy an organization's specific needs. ■ It is often difficult to integrate data from legacy systems or from external sources into data warehouse packages.	■ Review the capabilities of the package and your organization's specific needs. Make sure the fit is good. ■ Check references. Make sure that the package is not a prototype and that it has been used successfully by other organizations. ■ Make sure your IS department has addressed the issues related to data conversion and capacity. What are the conversion requirements to load existing data into the warehouse? Will the package handle all of the legacy data?

(Continued)

Table 9.3
Technology Checklist

Key Questions	Considerations
1. Does your organization have a systematic approach for evaluating technical options and for selecting vendors and tools?	■ There are numerous technical options, and it is not always immediately clear which option best fits the data or business problem.
2. Do the versions of the tools your organization has selected work together?	■ Most companies configure their data warehouses from an array of internal systems and purchased technologies. ■ Not all products work well with each other, even if they are sold by the same vendor. Different versions of tools from a single vendor's suite of products do not always integrate seamlessly.
3. Is your organization prepared (time and resources) to undergo technology conversions and/or upgrades?	■ Rapidly developing technologies and a consolidation of vendors and products can mandate unplanned upgrades or conversions.
4. Does your organization have personnel with the technical expertise needed to build a data warehouse?	■ The technologies are new, and the demands for skilled personnel are high. Organizations, including consulting firms, find it difficult to attract and retain knowledgeable personnel.

135

Table 9.4
Data Checklist

Key Questions	Considerations
1. Will developers be able to determine the information requirements?	■ There is no accepted methodology for determining information requirements for a data warehouse. ■ Developers often have to use empathic design techniques to design and implement a prototype. Then developers typically refine the original prototype numerous times.
2. Do you know your organization's requirements for historical data, and will your warehouse design accommodate your organization's historical data requirements?	■ Legal and/or regulatory considerations can mandate that large volumes of historical data be accessible in the warehouse. ■ The capacity of your data warehouse may not be adequate to include all of the required historical data.
3. If your organization will be assembling data for a warehouse from multiple sources, have you planned for converting and cleaning the data?	■ Many different conversion routines may be required. ■ Data may be of inconsistent and varying quality. ■ The quality of data in old legacy systems may be poor, and your organization may have to invest in a costly cleanup effort.
4. Has your organization reached consensus on the names, definitions, and sources of all data elements?	■ Unless there is total agreement, answers to queries and the queries themselves could be ambiguous.
5. Are the data your organization needs to load into the warehouse available through internal and/or external sources?	■ The current operational systems may not provide the required data. ■ The data may not be available through external sources.
6. If you will need to purchase external data from a vendor, do you have alternate sources identified?	■ Vendors can change data products, prices, and formats quickly, without adequate notification. Having a backup source for external data is a good risk management practice.

Table 9.4
Data Checklist *(Continued)*

Key Questions	Considerations
7. Have you established ownership of the data?	■ Organizations that have built data warehouses report that 70 to 80 percent of the warehouse effort was related to data issues. ■ Establishing ownership of the data minimizes these data issues.
8. Once the warehouse is built, will developers be prepared to prove the quality of the data to skeptical users?	■ Dirty data can undermine the credibility of responses to queries. ■ Designers need to be prepared to reconcile data back to the systems of record and to trace errors back to the structure of the query. ■ With multiple feeder systems, this reconciliation process can become very cumbersome.

Table 9.5
Organizational Checklist

Key Questions	Considerations
1. Does your organization have an evangelist with the energy, knowledge, and credibility to get a data warehouse project done?	■ Building data warehouses that deliver business value is a high-risk, high-reward activity that requires management commitment and technical know-how.
2. Does your data warehouse project have the endorsement and support from all areas of your IT organization, including the infrastructure, applications, and emerging technologies groups?	■ Data warehousing initiatives can legitimately be owned by any of several business units in and out of the IS unit. ■ Gaining support of all parties is a critical success factor.

Table 9.5
Organizational Checklist   *(Continued)*

Key Questions	Considerations
3. If you will be mining your warehouse, will analysts be taught discovery (inductive) processes in addition to hypothesis testing (deductive) processes?	▪ Skill development is critical for data mining.
4. Have you adequately addressed security and controls issues?	▪ Data warehouses, especially warehouses with sensitive or proprietary data about customers or products, have inherent control risks. (Information is consolidated and accessible for legitimate management queries and for potential misuse.)
5. Is your organization prepared to check the reasonableness of query responses and to prove the accuracy of the data?	▪ Data discovery can produce spurious results. ▪ Basing decisions on untested knowledge discovery is unwise.
6. Are complete training and support services provided for the business units that will be using the warehouse?	▪ Training is necessary, but not sufficient, to overcome people's reluctance to do hands-on reporting and analysis.
7. Does your warehouse training stress understanding the data?	▪ The tools are relatively easy; the data are difficult. ▪ Training too often focuses on using the query and reporting tools rather than understanding the definitions and structures of the data. ▪ Providing familiar tools (e.g., Excel for financial analysts) and semi-canned reports (e.g., point-and-click menu selections) facilitates hands-on use of the warehouse.
8. Does senior management have reasonable expectations regarding the benefits to be achieved from a data warehouse?	▪ It is too easy to oversell the benefits and the timing of the benefits.

Table 9.5
Organizational Checklist   *(Continued)*

Key Questions	Considerations
9. If your organization will be using a data warehouse to consolidate and integrate existing systems and/or organizations, have you carefully planned for change management?	▪ Consolidation and integration represent organizational change. ▪ Resistance should be expected.

Endnotes

1. Bashein, et al. *Safety Nets* (1997).
2. Ibid.

Annotated Bibliography

This bibliography provides references and summaries of relevant literature in two parts. Part 1 focuses explicitly on the technologies of data warehousing, data marts, and data mining. Part 2 examines other related literature with the ability to shed light on data warehousing issues.

1. Part 1 is divided into four subsections:

    a. The first describes how data, data mining, and data warehousing are used in organizations today.

    b. The second describes how data warehouses and data marts are designed and built.

    c. The third focuses on the vendors and their products.

    d. The fourth presents some of the best Web sites related to the topic.

2. Part 2 is divided into five subsections:

    a. The first deals with technologies that preceded or are similar to data warehousing and data marts, such as decision support systems and executive information systems.

    b. The second addresses strategic data planning.

    c. The third addresses how information requirements are to be determined.

    d. The fourth addresses knowledge discovery and individual and organizational learning.

    e. The fifth summarizes the issues involved in IT use by small businesses.

Part 1. Data Warehouses, Data Marts, and Data Mining

Uses of Data, Data Mining, and Data Warehousing

Baer, Tony. "Data Mart Users Try, Try Again." *Computerworld* (September 21, 1998): 67, 69.

Data marts at Dow Chemical "have paid for themselves in less than a year because their self-service reporting let Dow reduce its information technology reporting staff from 40 to five people." Political issues arise in development: Which organization has responsibility for which data?

Brachman, Ronald, J., Tom Khabaza, Willi Kloesgen, Gregory Piatetsky-Shapiro, and Evangelos Simoudis. "Mining Business Databases." *Communications of the ACM.* Vol. 39, no. 11 (November 1996): 42-48.

Data mining has two different goals: verification of a user's hypothesis, and discovery, the finding of new patterns in data. Discovery (sometimes referred to as knowledge discovery in databases, or KDD) includes prediction (regression and classification) and description (summarization, visualization, and detection of changes and deviations). Some KDD tools are generic; others are domain specific. Domain-specific tools represent an important trend—moving knowledge-discovering technology directly into the hands of business users. Among the elements that make this possible are putting the problem in the business user's terms, providing support for specific key business analyses, presenting results in a form geared to the business problem being solved, and providing support for a protracted iterative exploratory process. Data mining is only 15 to 25 percent of the overall KDD process. Knowledge discovery applications and prototypes have been developed for a variety of domains, including marketing, banking, telecommunications, and finance. The article discusses several specific tools for database marketing, financial investment, fraud detection, manufacturing and production, and network management.

Among the issues concerning the practical applications of KDD in industry are the following: Graduates of business schools are familiar with data analysis for verification but not with most discovery techniques. There is inadequate tool support for many discovery functions. Lack of business data integration hinders effective KDD. (Data warehousing is becoming widespread and can potentially alleviate the last problem.)

Bransten, Lisa. "Looking For Patterns." *The Wall Street Journal* (June 21, 1999): R16, R20.

"Data mining enables companies to better manage the reams of statistics they collect. The goal: spot the unexpected." The article describes one example where data mining shed light on the notion that drivers of high-performance sports cars are more likely to have accidents. Farmers Group discovered that as long as the sports car wasn't the only vehicle in the household, the accident rate wasn't much greater than that of a regular car. Thus, by letting Corvettes and Porsches into its preferred premium plan, Farmers estimated it could bring in an additional $4.5 million in premiums without a significant rise in claims. Other examples are also described.

The article cites studies by Forrester Research and Meta Group. Forrester found that only 28 percent of large companies were actively mining their databases, but all of the companies were planning to do so by 2001. Meta Group reports that corporate data warehouses are getting bigger. In 1996 only 6 percent were over a terabyte; in 1999 30 percent were over a terabyte. The article also highlights some of the barriers to data mining, including time, resources, and costs.

Davenport, Tom. "A Meeting of the Minds: Interview with Peter Drucker." *CIO* (September 15, 1997): 46-54.

Peter Drucker and Tom Davenport discuss topics surrounding the state of business and information management. Drucker stresses the importance of external information (a key component of successful data warehousing strategies). "The information you need the most—not just in business—is about the outside world, and there is absolutely none. It doesn't exist. You'd be surprised how much outside information about customers and noncustomers companies simply do not have and, in many cases, cannot get. And yet, you don't make your decisions on what goes on inside the company; you shouldn't at least" (p. 50).

Deck, Stewart. "Data Mining." *Computerworld* (March 29,1999): 76.

Data mining and data warehousing are related: Warehousing brings data together, and mining sorts through the data collected and turns up interesting and useful connections. The article defines data mining as "a process that finds relationships and patterns within a large amount of data stored in a database. The process uses tools based on algorithms to sift through mounds of data to find relationships." Warehouse analysis starts with a hypothesis and then pulls up data to support that theory. Data mining creates the theory.

DeSeve, Edward, Alvin M. Pesachowitz, and L. Kenneth Johnson. "Best IT Practices in the Federal Government." A Joint Project by the Chief Information Officers Council and the Industry Advisory Council (October 1997). http://www.cio.gov/docs/council.html.

This report contains a brief description of the Envirofacts Data Warehouse developed by the Environmental Protection Agency (EPA). This is one of the first successful large-scale data warehouse projects implemented at the federal level. This warehouse combines data from varied systems (e.g., Superfund, Hazardous Waste Handler). Information is made available to the public online at http://mountain.epa.gov/enviro/index.html. Difficulties encountered during development include lack of standard definitions of data elements, lack of a uniform IT architecture within EPA, and lack of in-house skills.

Drucker, Peter F. "The Future That Has Already Happened." *Harvard Business Review.* Vol. 75, no. 5 (September/October 1997): 20-24.

Drucker says that it is beneficial to identify major events that have already happened and that will have predictable effects in the next 10 to 20 years. He has some things to say, indirectly, about data warehousing. "Increasingly, a winning strategy will require information about events and conditions *outside* the institution: noncustomers, technologies other than those currently used by the company and its present competitors, markets not currently served, and so on. Only with this information can a business decide how to allocate its knowledge resources in order to produce the highest yield. Only with such information can a business also prepare for new changes and challenges arising from sudden shifts in the world economy....The development of rigorous methods for gathering and analyzing outside information will increasingly become a major challenge for businesses and for information experts" (p. 22).

Fabris, Peter. "A Civilian Action." *CIO Magazine Section 1* (February 1, 1998): 52-65.

Presents a useful short case of the EnviroFacts data warehouse at EPA.

Fabris, Peter. "Advanced Navigation." *CIO Section 1* (May 15, 1998): 50-55.

Presents a useful short case of data mining in the banking industry.

Fayyad, Usama, and Ramasamy Uthurusamy (guest editors). "Data Mining and Knowledge Discovery in Databases." *Communications of the ACM.* Vol. 39, no. 11 (November 1996): 24-26.

The authors describe the problem to which data mining is the solution as "now that we have gathered so much data, what do we do with it?" The true value of data is predicated on the ability to extract from it information useful for decisionmaking and understanding the phenomena underlying the data. A community of researchers and practitioners interested in the problem of automating data analysis is growing, known as KDD.

Fayyad, Usama, Gregory Piatetsky-Shapiro, and Padhraic Smyth. "The KDD Process for Extracting Useful Knowledge from Volumes of Data." *Communications of the ACM.* Vol. 39, no. 11 (November 1996): 27-34.

This article provides a great tutorial on data mining and related topics.

The ability to analyze and understand massive datasets lags far behind the ability to gather and store the data. Examples of large databases include grocery store check-out data, bank credit card authorization data, and telephone call data. The traditional method of turning data into knowledge relies on manual analysis and interpretation, summarized in a written report. Manual analysis is slow, expensive, and subjective; it is becoming impractical in many domains as data volumes grow exponentially. People are looking to computer technology to automate the data analysis process. Although this problem is not new, automation in the context of large databases opens up many new unsolved problems.

The term KDD is used in this article to describe the overall process of discovering useful knowledge from data. KDD consists of many steps, of which "data mining," a term commonly used by statisticians, MIS specialists, and businesspeople, is only one (application of specific algorithms for extracting patterns from data). The process includes the following steps: learning the application domain, creating a target dataset, data cleaning and preprocessing, data reduction and projection (incorporation of appropriate prior knowledge), data mining (choosing the function of data mining, choosing the algorithms, mining the data), proper interpretation of the results of mining, and using the discovered knowledge (includes documenting and taking action). Blind application of data mining methods can lead to the discovery of meaningless patterns and therefore misdirect decisionmakers. Data warehousing refers to the current business trend of collecting and cleaning transactional data to make them available for online analysis. KDD is defined as "the nontrivial process of identifying valid, novel, potentially useful, and ultimately understandable patterns in data." (The term "pattern" includes models and data structures.)

Data mining algorithms largely consist of some mix of three components: the model (contains parameters that are to be determined from the data), the preference criterion (basis for preferring one model or set of parameters over another, e.g., goodness of fit), and the search algorithm (a way to find a particular model instance and parameters given data, model, and preference criterion). In current data mining practice, models commonly serve the following functions: classification, regression, clustering, summarization, dependency modeling, link analysis, and sequence analysis.

The article concludes with a set of research issues and challenges, some of which reflect practitioners' problems. Among these are reducing the hardware requirements of massive datasets; dealing with missing data resulting from human error, system and measurement failures, and revision of data collection procedures; increasing the understandability of the patterns found in data; integrating KDD with other organizational systems; and dealing with nonstandard data (e.g., multimedia). One very important problem is assisting the nonexpert user in the proper selection and matching of tools and technique to achieve their goals. Many current KDD methods and tools are not truly interactive and do not easily incorporate prior knowledge about a problem except in simple ways.

Fox, Bruce. "IT on the Cheap." *RT (Retailtech)* (August 1997): 2-24, 26.

Retail grocery chain Trader Joe's does not capture point-of-sale information at the item level. It professes to have no use for data warehousing. And it claims to spend just 0.2 percent of its revenues on MIS, compared to a retail industry average of 1.5 percent. Trader Joe's claims that older processes can achieve most of the objectives of data warehousing more inexpensively. Although these technologies do not enable the chain to make ad hoc queries, Trader Joe's can identify important queries and write programs to answer them.

Gartner, Gideon. "Grappling With e.Knowledge." *Computerworld* (December 29, 1997/January 5, 1998): 43.

Gartner identifies a need to improve IT awareness in the president's office and questions whether presidents are sufficiently IT aware to be frustrated with the lack of accessible decision-support data. He identifies a growing institutional recognition of knowledge management, exemplified by advances in data warehousing that plan for later intelligent use of information. The difference between information and knowledge is based on value—knowledge is usually relevant to decisions and therefore carries more value.

Gartner claims that the volume of information is staggering relative to our capacity to absorb it. "Solutions to the glut problem must employ technology to abstract (or highlight) and synthesize multiple hits from searches....e.knowledge is the application of electronic technologies to the creation, classification, synthesis, analysis, storage, retrieval and display of knowledge."

Hagel III, John, and Jeffrey F. Rayport. "The Coming Battle for Customer Information." *McKinsey Quarterly.* No. 3 (1997): 64-76.

Collecting information about customers can yield many benefits, such as enabling a company to target prospects more effectively and tailor products and services to customer needs. However, this article argues, customers are becoming increasingly aware of the value of their information to the companies that collect it and are reluctant to sell it cheaply. You can expect customers to demand considerations like discounts and frequent-shopper points for providing information. In addition, there are new opportunities for "infomediaries" (companies that act as custodians, agents, brokers, and marketers of customer information).

Hagel III, John, and A.M. Sacconaghi, Jr. "Who Will Benefit From Virtual Information?" *McKinsey Quarterly.* No. 3 (1996): 22-37.

The most useful information about consumers, such as when they are about to make a purchase or how much they are buying from competitors, has often been inaccessible to marketers. Today, with the emergence of online markets, this information may become available, offering significant new opportunities to create new value. The question is, who will be able to capture this value? The more information is collected about consumers, the more privacy becomes a potential issue. It may be that information intermediaries will capture much of the value through their perceived ability to safeguard consumer privacy. More important is the question of the extent to which customer concerns about privacy will lead to restrictions on the use of captured information.

Haley, Barbara J., Watson, Hugh J., and Goodhue, Dale L. "The Benefits of Data Warehousing at Whirlpool." *Idea Group Publishing Cases* (no date): www.idea-group.com/casesam.htm.

Whirlpool uses data warehousing for quality tracking and supply chain management. Engineers use it to track performance of component parts: 16 million appliances are made each year and tracked throughout their lifetimes. A prior executive information system initiative had been discontinued. The first data warehousing effort was approved in 1993. Today the data warehouse contains 14 specific collections of data (subject areas). Data warehousing is viewed as an infrastructure investment, with benefits coming from subsequent applications. Therefore, the company used blanket approvals and no post-implementation audit. Marketing users access data marts (not the warehouse itself) and use simple PowerBuilder interface access tools. New employees are educated during orientation, with additional courses as needed. The support team consists of six members and people in local units.

Inmon, W.H. "The Data Warehouse and Data Mining." *Communications of the ACM.* Vol. 39, no. 11 (November 1996): 49-50.

The data warehouse sets the stage for effective data mining. It greatly increases the chances of data mining success. A data warehouse includes integrated data, detailed and summarized data, historical data, and meta-data (data about data). OLAP data marts are an extension of data warehouses. Data mining at the data warehouse is primary data mining because of the elemental nature of the data, while data mining at an OLAP data mart can be considered secondary data mining.

Kempster, Lisa. "ERP, Warehouse Used in Concert." *Computerworld* (September 21, 1998): 67, 69.

This article is about the nation's largest seller of snowboards, Burton Snowboards in Burlington, Vermont. SAP solved half of the growing company's reporting problems. Transaction data from three offices were captured and collected in a central data warehouse. But the company soon found that, if it needed to run any nonstandard reporting on the SAP system, the IS staff couldn't handle the effort because it was too small for that level of complexity. Today, Burton uses an OLAP reporting database. Most of the executives and 70 percent of the middle managers use the system hands-on without IS department intervention.

Neary, Ryan. "Building a Data Warehouse and Data Mining for a Strategic Advantage." *Journal of Information Technology Theory and Application.* Vol. 1, no. 1 (1999): http://www.jitta.org/

This readable tutorial on data warehousing and mining is available online at http://clam.rutgers.edu/~ejournal/spring99/Manu3.htm.

Pass, Stephen. "Discovering Value in a Mountain of Data." *OR/MS Today.* Vol. 24, no. 5 (October 1997): 24-28.

Among the applications that can benefit from data mining are promotion analysis, category management, logistics and distribution analysis, trend analysis, claims analysis, sales and profitability analysis, customer profiling, churn analysis, rate and usage analysis, forecasting, budget analysis, target mailing list identification, data validation, and fraud detection.

Data mining is seen as a potential solution to information overload: being so busy analyzing the data that one doesn't have the time to do anything creative with the results. On top of that is the unquantifiable benefit of improved morale among staff, who now have time for more creative endeavors.

Data mining methods differ from statistical analysis methods. Most data are nonlinear and not well addressed by traditional statistical tools. Among the data mining methods are neural networks (nonlinear predictive models that learn from data), decision trees, genetic algorithms, fuzzy logic, and hybrid approaches.

Slater, Derek. "What Have You Done with IT Lately?" *CIO* (September 15, 1997): 114-120.

This article reports the results of a survey conducted by *CIO* and investment bank Morgan Stanley, Dean Witter, Discover & Co., asking high-level executives (mostly IS executives at large corporations) about their current technology portfolios and budgeting plans. "Data mining was the technology most soundly cuffed by the companies surveyed.... However, ...a fairly high percentage said they are evaluating data mining 'since they hear a lot of noise about it.'"

The levels of technology use for data warehousing/data marts are reported as 21 percent full production/standard, 36 percent implementation under way, 11 percent plan to purchase within 12 months, 24 percent currently evaluating, and 16 percent not considering. By industry, respondents using data warehousing/data marts at full production/standard level are reported as 25 percent finance, 22 percent manufacturing, 33 percent business services/consulting,

24 percent government/military, 11 percent health care, 24 percent retail/wholesale, and 45 percent telecommunications.

Stedman, Craig. "Data Vaults Unlocked: External Users Gain Access to Info Over the Web." *Computerworld* (June 2, 1997): 1, 17.

Companies are beginning to fulfill customers' requests to gain access to warehoused data about themselves via the Internet. One example is a distributor of medical and surgical supplies that began to extract purchase history files from its data warehouse and send them to key customers who wanted to analyze their spending. A network of hospitals could use the information to reduce costs by standardizing purchases across the group. The article highlights the benefits of Web-based warehousing:

- Tightens relationships with customers.

- Helps keep them from switching to other suppliers.

- Reduces the need for paper-based reports.

The article also highlights the hurdles:

- Need to ensure outsiders see only their own data.

- Unclear whether customers will help foot the bill.

- Lack of Web-based tools with full query capabilities

Stedman, Craig. "Data Mining for Fool's Gold." *Computerworld* (December 1, 1997): 1, 28.

This article highlights the risks of incorrect discoveries from data mining. Although data mining tools can unearth valuable findings, they can also turn out spurious, statistically invalid, and trivial findings. For example, one data mining exercise found a strong historical link between the rise and fall of the S&P 500 stock index and butter production in Bangladesh. Mistakes can be dangerous. One large bank got a faulty reading on the average balances of some credit card customers because data had been posted incorrectly.

Frequently, 99 percent of a mining tool's findings turn out to be obvious, irrelevant, or flawed. Some safety tips for would-be data miners include:

- Shop carefully for tools. There are more than 50 vendors.

- Get business people involved, not just statisticians. Getting useful results out of data mining requires detailed knowledge of the data.
- Neatness counts for data. Unclean or inconsistent data contribute to incorrect discoveries.
- Don't be vague; ask specific business-oriented questions.
- Check findings for statistical validity.
- Don't expect miracles. Using data mining tools takes a lot of effort.

The tools need to be handled carefully; the data need to be cleaned meticulously, and the results need to be checked tediously. The author underscores the importance of the human element and the problem in finding people with the requisite mix of business and statistical analysis skills.

Stedman, Craig. "Data Warehouse Despite the Dangers." *Computerworld* (January 5, 1998): 61-62.

Although data mining can produce discoveries that turn out to be spurious, many organizations are realizing benefits. Charles Schwab & Co., for example, predicts trading patterns and focuses its marketing by segmenting customers into groups based on investment experience and willingness to take risks. Schwab's analysts reportedly spend 80 percent of their time prepping data and laboriously testing the mining results for accuracy.

Another example is Chase Manhattan's Consumer Credit unit. Data mining disproved conventional wisdom that people with multiple accounts were bound to be the bank's best customers. Chase Manhattan discovered that many customers with multiple accounts were unprofitable and modified its approach to cross-selling accounts.

Stedman, Craig. "Data Warehouses Make ERP Whole." *Computerworld* (November 30, 1998): 55, 58.

Data warehouses are "turning out to be the glue that holds everything together." The article talks about several companies that are using data warehouses as connecting layers for disparate ERP systems or for uniform, but far-flung, ERP systems.

The article includes the results of a survey taken by The Data Warehousing Institute, where a question was asked: What kind of technology do you plan to use to warehouse and analyze your ERP data? The responses were as follows (note that multiple responses were allowed):

■ Stand-alone data warehouse (61 percent).

■ Report writers built into ERP software (56 percent).

■ Third-party query tools tied to ERP system (31 percent).

■ ERP vendor's data warehousing software (27 percent).

Wreden, Nick. "Business Boosting Technologies." *Beyond Computing* (November/December 1997): 27-32.

The author reports the results of a survey of corporate and technology management on which technologies will have the greatest impact on business in 1998. Surprisingly, there was consistency between the IT and business executives on why and how to deploy technology resources.

The primary drivers for implementing new technologies in 1998 were productivity improvements (51 percent), cost reductions (39 percent), improving decisionmaking (36 percent), managing/enhancing customer relationships (33 percent), and developing new strategic applications (33 percent). The technologies that will have the greatest impact on business in 1998 were Internet (54 percent), client/server (43 percent), data warehousing/data mining/OPAP (30 percent), intranets/extranets (28 percent), and network computing (24 percent).

Awareness of the strategic and competitive advantages of data warehousing appeared to be broad, with 58 percent of the citings coming from business managers and 42 percent coming from IT managers. One respondent noted that employees who can see and feel the data will be able to make better-informed decisions than competitors.

Zerega, Blaise. "American Airlines Accountants Earn Wings," *Infoworld* (April 6, 1998): 99.

"At American Airlines, the revenue accounting department smashed the stereotype of end-users depending on an IT department to generate reports. Instead, accountants gained a working knowledge of SQL and now create ad hoc queries from a 300GB data mart." Building the system required several months of raking through data and looking for corrupted indexes. It has 20 tables, with an average query time of seven minutes (40 percent of queries arc completed in less than four minutes.) A two-day training course is given. ROI for the warehouse exceeded expectations and saved $60,000 by spotting improper ticketing procedures.

Zornes, Aaron. "Off-Road Access: To Provide Web Access to Data Warehouses, You'll Have to Explore the Terrain Beyond the Beaten Track." *CIO Section 1* (November 15, 1997): 26, 30.

The Social Security Administration's Web-enabled data repository failed because the public did not think it secure. But executives are rushing ahead because the business case for Web-enablement is solid.

Designing and Building Data Warehouses and Marts

Atre, Shaku. "No Panaceas." *Computerworld* (December 15, 1997): 67, 70.

The author highlights the importance of corporate politics in setting the strategic direction for data warehousing. Rather than building enterprise data warehouses that require business units to cooperate and share data, companies often choose to build stand-alone data marts. When they do not understand the benefits of enterprise data warehouses, senior executives do not get involved to resolve the organizational problems.

The decision-support needs of the entire business should be considered before making a decision to implement data marts or a data warehouse or both. If the decision favors data marts, the data marts should be implemented within an enterprise strategy.

Atre, Shaku. "Elusive Productivity." *Computerworld* (November 17, 1997): 83, 86.

This article addresses the issue of how to justify a data warehouse to senior management. A data warehouse can strengthen control by improving decision support. Actionable information can be extracted from reorganized versions of the operational data businesses already collect and can be blended with external data, which can illuminate the internal data. Data warehousing can be a diagnostic tool to spot and interpret trends.

Atre, Shaku. "The Trouble with Training." *Computerworld* (October 20, 1997): 73, 76.

Data warehousing faces many of the same challenges and problems as client/server systems. They both:

- Rely on new concepts and processes that are not easily understood by users or technical staff.
- Have graphical user interfaces (GUIs) that look easy to use. But product training is necessary.
- Are often built by departmental users who rebel against IS. They may produce disparate, multivendor systems that require a proliferation of support tools.
- Have risen rapidly and use new products that need frequent upgrading.
- Tend to cost more and take longer than expected.
- Use iterative design methodologies instead of traditional waterfall techniques. Developers may not have a grasp of all the steps needed to get a system up and running.
- Require planning and formal data modeling.
- Face challenges in dealing with legacy data.

Demarest, Marc. "The Politics of Data Warehousing." DPA Inc., White Paper (January 1998): http://www.dpapplications.com/i0700.html.

Data warehousing projects are frequently sidetracked by organizational politics. Therefore, designers have to adopt new work practices to optimize the chances for successful data warehouse deployment. The paper explains that data warehousing projects are always potentially political because they cross organizational treaty lines; they change both the terms of data ownership and data access, exposing the often-checkered history of data management in the IT organization; and they affect the work practices of highly autonomous and powerful user communities in the firm. Danger signs of political activity are identified (e.g., "people inside and outside the project team talking about the data warehousing primarily or exclusively in terms of technology components"). Countermeasures that data warehouse designers can take to increase the chances of success are listed (e.g., "do the sociological analysis first").

Gardner, Stephen R. "Building the Data Warehouse." *Communications of the ACM.* Vol. 41, no. 9 (September 1998): 52-60.

According to the author, "data warehousing is a process, not a product, for assembling and managing data from various sources for the purpose of gaining a single, detailed view of part or all of a business." Data warehousing includes (1) enterprise data warehouses, (2) independent data marts, and (3) dependent data marts.

The article includes diagrams and descriptions of a data warehouse framework and a data warehouse methodology, which together provide some guidelines for implementing a data warehouse.

Glassey, Katherine. "Seducing the End User." *Communications of the ACM.* Vol. 41, no. 9 (September 1998): 62-69.

"The key to generating the ROI corporate management expects from data warehousing projects is a design that inspires end users to actually use the solution." The author advocates "user-centric" warehousing. Users need to be able to access data any time, anywhere. They want to run queries over the Web and then manipulate and analyze the data while flying to business meetings. The author, who is a cofounder and the chief technology officer of Brio Technology, Inc., describes user-centric warehousing concepts in terms of Brio's products.

Gray, Paul, and Hugh Watson. *Decision Support in the Data Warehouse.* Upper Saddle River, NJ: Prentice Hall PTR, 1998.

This book is the latest in the Data Warehousing Institute Series from Prentice Hall PTR. In addition to an overview of the new decision support environment, the book covers creating the data warehouse, supporting decisions in the data warehouse, and products for decision support. (This last part contains product descriptions by Oracle, Red Brick Systems, Brio Technology, and others.)

Data warehousing involves placing specially prepared data on computer platforms separate from transaction processing systems to support decisionmaking. This approach provides easy and speedy access and improves data integrity and security. Some of the key characteristics of data warehouses include containing data that are cleaned (accurate and accessible via a single, consistent referencing convention); providing time series data (five to 10 years, versus 60 to 90 days for operational databases); and containing detail data, summarized data, and meta-data (data about data). Organizations need data warehouses for performance, data access, data formats, and data quality. A data mart is a small warehouse designed for a strategic business unit or department.

The part on creating the data warehouse reviews technical fundamentals (e.g., data modeling) and the process of building and maintaining a warehouse. Business needs for data warehouses include the need to create a single version of the truth, the need to automate data collection and updating, and the need to offload analysis and reporting functions from transaction processing systems. Data warehousing is most used in marketing for trend analyses, buying patterns, and sales promotions. Among the critical success factors in data warehousing are setting specific, achievable, measurable goals; involving all stakeholders; keeping a big-picture perspective; attending to assumptions and details; considering long-term strategy for the warehouse; and learning from others. The various design decisions involved in constructing a data warehouse are reviewed.

The decision support part of the book covers tools (e.g., OLAP, SQL, intranets, data mining tools), applications development (requirements determination, software selection, data management), and additional considerations. Among the pitfalls noted are losing sight of the business problem, failing to ensure data quality, failing to manage data extraction and transformation; being unable to coordinate data marts; and lacking scalability. Use of consultants is common because organizations lack data warehousing and mining experience. The Web browser is becoming the primary vehicle for access to warehoused data. Determining data requirements is still a black art.

Greengard, Samuel. "How Do You Build a Data Warehouse Solution?" *Beyond Computing* (March 1999): 18, 20, 22.

This article describes companies that have assembled warehouse solutions "from a mix of warehouses, marts and legacy databases, combined with the right software." These hybrid solutions link new and existing systems, using a mix of data warehouse and data marts for different platforms. The article includes some tips from the Data Warehousing Institute:

1. Establish a collaborative relationship with end users and executives.

2. Start small and grow the warehouse incrementally.

3. Source data from fewer systems to minimize the political risk of trying to define data elements consistently across application areas.

4. Since warehouses expose inaccurate data, fix inaccuracies at both the front end and the back end.

Koch, Christopher. "The Middle Ground: Will Dependent Data Marts Strike a Balance between Huge Data Warehouse Rollouts and Piecemeal Data Mart Implementations?" *CIO Section 1* (January 15, 1999): 49-54.

According to a 1997 survey by Meta Group, Inc., companies spent an average of $1.9 million on data warehousing projects. This article emphasizes that these projects involve "unprecedented levels of technical difficulty and painful organizational change." Another report from Meta Group states that 50 percent of these multimillion-dollar projects fail to meet the desired levels of success among IS groups. Many CIOs fail in their first and second attempts at creating successful data warehouses.

Size is an important factor; both extremes have drawbacks. Large, enterprisewide warehouses are difficult to build and maintain. Small, narrowly focused data marts "present no incentives to share information with the rest of the company and can lead to a chaos of incompatible technologies, duplicate data and an overwhelming demand for system maintenance."

A hybrid approach (called dependent data marts) emerges "that combines a central data warehouse (to reduce IS's support nightmare) with many smaller data marts that pull data through the data warehouse so that everyone uses identically formatted data in their calculations." This approach can reduce IS support and improve access to data for the business units. Cost studies support the hybrid approach, which is less expensive to build and maintain than other approaches.

LaPlante, Alice. "Eternal Project." *Computerworld* (July 13 1998): 61, 62.

This article emphasizes "the surprising—and inevitable—fact that a warehouse is never, ever really finished." Five challenges are identified and discussed:

1. Your business changes. Your warehouse must change with it. Early warning signs include a backlog of requests for modifications.

2. The technology changes. "Technology advances that allow for greater productivity, efficiency and cost savings might force necessary changes."

3. Keeping your IT workers interested. While IT workers want to build warehouses, they may not want to maintain them.

4. Easy-to-use tools aren't, users complain. Users may have a different perspective on what's easy to use.

5. Dirty or out-of-sync data. The risk here is that users get answers to their queries that don't make sense to them. "They lose confidence, they get suspicious, and the warehouse dies."

Lehmann, Peter, and Johann Jaszewski. "Business Terms as a Critical Success Factor for Data Warehousing." Proceedings of the International Workshop on Design and Management of Data Warehouses, Heidelberg, Germany. June 14-15, 1999: http//sunsite.informatik. rwth-aachen.de/Publications/CEUR-WS/Vol-19/

This paper describes a practical approach to providing high-quality data by clarifying the meanings of various business terms. The approach was developed at Lawson Mardon Singen, a German supplier of flexible packaging materials.

Moad, Jeff. "Buried Information Treasure." *PCWeek Online* (October 13, 1997): http://www.zdnet.com/pcweek/news/1013/13erp.html.

Managers have been surprised at how difficult it can be to unlock critical data captured in so-called ERP suites.

Moad, Jeff. "Tips for Moving R/3 Data to Warehouses." *PCWeek Online* (October 13, 1997): http://www.zdnet.com/pcweek/news/1013/13tips.html.

Should you try building your own data warehouse by writing your own programs to extract SAP R/3 data? If you head down that path without first doing some careful planning, you're likely to run into problems.

Paul, Gibbons Lauren. "Anatomy of a Failure: The Inside Story of a Fatally Flawed Data Warehouse Project." *CIO Enterprise Section 2* (November 15, 1997): 55-60.

The CEO of a telemarketing company got data warehousing religion on the golf course with a software vendor. Rapid growth of the company had put pressures on the company's existing systems. Other growth plans made it a bad year for technology projects. The IS staff was stretched and had no warehousing experience, so five outsiders were hired. Managers were not sold on the idea; they were happy with canned reports. Says consultant: challenges go up dramatically if the data warehouse is the first analytical environment. The CEO stuck to tight schedule costs despite consultant pushback. The project lacked clearly defined business objectives. No group meeting of the sponsors was held. Performance of customer service representatives was subjective and hard to measure. There were no common definitions of key business concepts. There were delays getting agreement, and IS folks thought the data warehouse threatened their jobs. They claimed there was no way to get the data to populate the warehouse. A solution was jury-rigged, but without rewriting transaction systems, no long-term solution was possible. Users didn't accept the warehouse: "We've already got a solution," they said. The CIO left. It was later estimated to take two years to reengineer the core systems for a proper data warehouse.

Porter, John D., and John J. Rome. "Lessons from a Successful Data Warehouse Implementation." *Cause/Effect* (Winter 1995): 43-50.

This article describes a case study of data warehousing at Arizona State University. Making official numbers available in a data warehouse brings consistency and credibility. Delivering "officialness" is not as easy as it sounds. The programs that extract and transform data from legacy databases must produce numbers that balance with official numbers. Since different algorithms and extract programs exist, the data warehouse and the official university reports often differ. The problem multiplies because of 10 years of data in the warehouse. Creating and validating 10 years of official data was difficult. Going forward in time was easier. One lesson learned was to avoid cost justification. Gartner Group reports claim tangible benefits will come, but how can such benefits be quantified?

Rodero, José A., José A. Toval, and Mario G. Piattini. "The Audit of the Data Warehouse Framework." Proceedings of the International Workshop on Design and Management of Data Warehouses, Heidelberg, Germany, June 14-15, 1999: http//sunsite.informatik.rwth-aachen.de/Publications/CEUR-WS/Vol-19/.

This paper describes important aspects of the control systems needed in data warehousing initiatives and a methodology for the data warehouse audit process.

SAS Institute World Headquarters (Cary, NC), *A SAS Institute White Paper: Rapid Warehousing Methodology* (no date).

This paper stresses the interview process during the requirements-gathering phase of a warehouse project. "As part of the planning meeting, we introduce an Interview Process to define user requirements more precisely. A series of interviews will be held with senior management, user management, end users of the data warehouse, and the IT department. These interviews will form the bulk of all input to the main Phase 2 deliverable—the data warehouse Requirements Definitions Document. The Requirements Definition

Document provides a detailed outline of the end-users' business needs, the IT department's architecture/strategy needs, subject definitions(s), data warehouse logical and physical models, transformation models, and a scope of work for implementation. A well-executed interview process is important for the success of the data warehouse implementation."

Spinner, Karen. "Going Down to the Data Mart." *CFO* (December 1997): www.cfonet.com.

Data warehouses were supposed to be the ultimate system solution. But warehouses became so large that they stretched the limits of hardware storage and software response times. Thus, data marts have gained in popularity.

A data mart is a special-purpose database that contains the portion of a data warehouse that is of interest to a particular group of users. Data marts, typically less than 50 gigabytes of data, address a specific function and are usually faster and less costly to implement than full-scale data warehouses ($200,000 and two months compared to $3 million and three years). Because of the reduced time and cost, data mart projects are less risky than enterprise data warehouse projects, which strain corporate IT functions.

Benefits of data marts include more rapid access to task-specific information and more flexible data formatting. Data marts are particularly useful for financial analysis, including economic value-added and activity-based costing. But the summarized data in data marts has limitations for power users who want to drill down to the transaction level.

To address the scalability issues, some organizations use data marts as an intermediate step in building enterprise data warehouses. A collection of relational data marts fed by legacy systems may in turn be used to feed a data warehouse. With multiple sources of data, an organization needs a data model or meta-data (data about data) layer. Vendors offer tool kits (data marts in a box) to facilitate developing and maintaining multiple-source data marts. These tools include a firm-wide meta-data layer to manage information stored in one or more data marts.

Another approach is to use prefab data marts that draw on a data warehouse. These marts are automatically updated as the source database is updated.

Finance departments can implement a multidimensional data mart without a great deal of involvement from the IT organization. Products available include both a data model that can be used to build and populate a multidimensional database and a suite of financial reporting and flexible query tools. Finance users can create their own reports rather than ask the IT group to build custom programs for reports not included in the canned library (with an extensive library of canned reports, only 20 percent of the required reports are not included). In developing a multidimensional database, it is important to identify up front how the group wants to slice and dice data—e.g., time period, cost center, planned quantity, actual quantity, organizational hierarchy, and order hierarchy.

The independent data mart approach runs the risk of creating islands of data. Some businesses address this risk by building enterprise data warehouses one data mart at a time. Tool kits are becoming available that facilitate implementing distributed or networked data marts with centralized meta-data. Web access to data marts is also becoming a requirement for finance executives.

Stedman, Craig. "Companies Rope in Wayward Data Marts." *Computerworld* (September 1, 1997): 24.

This article reports that the pendulum is swinging from stand-alone data marts back toward centralized data warehouses. Businesses are beginning to overlay existing marts with a corporate warehousing framework in order to give users consistent access to information. The risk is that different systems produce reports giving different answers to the same question.

Data marts can be built quickly and can give users faster query responses than a data warehouse. But a collection of inconsistent data marts creates management difficulties and blocks users from running queries across the full spectrum of corporate data. Businesses report that stovepipe data marts were a worthwhile investment to promote the concept of data warehousing, but they are now establishing a warehousing architecture, consolidating overlapping data marts, and offloading feeds from production systems to a central staging database. The article includes some rules for building data marts from the Gartner Group:

- Set up separate data warehouse and data mart teams.
- Set guidelines to head off redundant development work.
- Ensure that data marts can be fed by a central warehouse.
- Define policies to limit data mart proliferation.

Stedman, Craig. "Data Warehouse Nightmare: Mergers Cause Major Headaches for IS, End Users." *Computerworld* (May 19, 1997): 1, 16.

This article points out some of the difficulties faced by IS organizations when companies involved in mergers and acquisitions want to merge their data warehouses. One example involves FHP International Corp., which was bought by PacifiCare Health Systems, Inc. The data warehouse merger hurdles are summarized. For IS, the hurdles are:

- Different databases, hardware, and warehousing tools.
- Incompatible data models and database designs.
- Warehouses that focus on different types of information.
- Inconsistent terminology and table entry formats.

For end users, the hurdles are:

- Functions that may not be supported in new warehouse.
- A need to learn new data definitions and terms.
- Database design changes that force new navigation methods.
- Potential need to switch query and reporting tools.

Stedman, Craig. "Luring Users Into the Warehouse: Gathering Their Requirements Is Key." *Computerworld* (June 2, 1997): 47, 49.

The risk of omitting input from end users is that a data warehouse will not meet business needs. Three key challenges in soliciting user input are:

- Finding business users with free time is difficult.

- Different business units may have conflicting ideas of what they want from a data warehouse.
- Users often do not know what they want.

Traditional IS techniques for gathering user requirements may not work. IS professionals may have to locate a small number of interested users and then dig deeper into the business process than they typically do.

Watson, Hugh J., and Barbara J. Haley. "Managerial Considerations." *Communications of the ACM.* Vol. 41, no. 9 (September 1998): 32-37.

The authors report results from their research program in data warehousing. Their most interesting and important findings center around how organizations gain approval for data warehousing projects, how data warehouses are implemented, and what post-implementation issues should be addressed.

Post-implementation benefits are sustained when the business units get involved and stay involved. "Organizations that fail to provide sufficient business-unit support begin to see informal user support contracts. This arrangement leads to inefficiency, because power users do less of their own work as they spend time solving the problems of their less technically savvy colleagues."

Whiting, Rick. "Warehouse ROI: Data Warehouses Are Getting the Same Scrutiny as Other Projects." *Information Week* (May 24, 1999): 99, 102, 104.

In the past, data warehouse projects have often been exempt from ROI or payback analysis. "As late as 1997, a Forrester Research survey found that only 16 of 50 companies were conducting any kind of dollar-based ROI measurements before implementing a data warehouse." But things may be changing. The trend is to apply some of the same payback and ROI analyses that govern most capital expenditures. Attaching a dollar figure to benefits, however, is difficult. For a warehouse to yield benefits, someone has to act on the findings from the warehouse. And quantifying indirect benefits (such as improved customer retention) may be impossible.

APPENDIX A

Vendors and Products

Atre Associates, Inc. "The Data Warehouse/Data Mart Navigator." *Computerworld* Special Fold-Out Poster (September 22, 1997).

This fold-out poster, a visual tool with color graphics for data warehouse/data mart implementation, gives an overview of the numerous vendors and products. The poster identifies and describes 12 implementation steps:

1. Determining users' needs.
2. Determining the database management system (DBMS) Server Platform.
3. Determining hardware platform.
4. Information and data modeling.
5. Constructing the meta-data repository.
6. Data acquisition and cleansing.
7. Transformation, transportation, population.
8. Determining middleware connectivity.
9. Prototyping, querying, and reporting.
10. Data mining.
11. Online analytical processing.
12. Deployment and systems management.

Then the steps are divided into appropriate product categories (e.g., step 9 is divided into ad hoc queries and reports and advanced queries and reports). Each product category has an accompanying menu of vendors who provide products or services appropriate for that step.

Bontempo, Charles, and George Zagelow. "The IBM Data Warehouse Architecture." *Communications of the ACM.* Vol. 41, no. 9 (September 1998): 38-48.

This article describes IBM's comprehensive set of data warehouse components (hardware and software), which can be integrated with each other and/or with other vendors' tools. The authors discuss "the importance of design features enabling tight integration of data warehouse components to simplify deployment and administration." (Note that Zagelow is an IBM employee.) Tables and figures (e.g., one titled "A visual warehouse implementation," which includes products from numerous vendors) provide a framework for understanding some of the integration issues.

Foley, John. "Focused Mining: Marketing and Data Mining Tools Are Married for Targeted Drilling." *Information Week* (November 24, 1997): 87.

This article reports on another instance of data warehousing vendors (SAS Institute, Inc. and Exchange Applications, Inc.) integrating their products. The two vendors have many customers in common. SAS's Interprise Miner uses a variety of modeling techniques to find patterns among warehoused data. Exchange Applications' ValEx manages direct marketing campaigns, including dividing customers into segments for targeted marketing, executing a marketing campaign, and evaluating the results. Better-integrated products will allow analysts to spend more time on analysis and less on linkage issues.

Foley, John. "OLAP Spreads: Vendors Are Integrating Online Analytical Processing With Enterprise Applications." *Information Week* (October 20, 1997): 20-22.

Online analytical processing was used mainly by power users in financial departments for intense number crunching. Now OLAP products are becoming more available and more suitable for mainstream users. Rather than the two-dimensional tables of relational databases, OLAP products arrange data in multidimensional cubes. This arrangement is both more intuitive for users and more efficient for some calculations.

Vendors include Arbor, Cognos, Comshare, Hyperion, IBM, Informix, Microsoft, and Oracle. IBM is adding an OLAP layer (based on Arbor's Essbase) to its DB2 relational database. Oracle is upgrading its Oracle Applications Data Warehouse, which populates data warehouses with data from Oracle's packaged applications. Microsoft is adding OLAP capabilities to Excel, Visual Basic, and SQL Server database.

ERP software vendors are integrating OLAP tools with their products, too. Baan is using Hyperion software, and PeopleSoft is using Essbase.

Foley, John, with Joy D. Russell. "Best From Data: Online Analytical Processing and Data Mining Offer Top-down and Bottom-up Value." *Information Week* (January 5, 1998): 88-89.

Two hot-selling technologies this year will be online analytical processing and data mining. OLAP facilitates top-down data analysis, and data mining facilitates bottom-up data discovery. The markets in both areas are projected to grow significantly, according to *The OLAP Report* and the Meta Group (for OLAP from about $1 billion in 1996 to more than $3 billion in 2000, and for data mining from $3.3 billion in 1996 to $8.4 billion in 2000).

OLAP servers organize data into multidimensional hierarchies, or cubes, for high-speed data analysis. IBM, Microsoft, and Sybase are expected to introduce OLAP options for their relational databases; Oracle and Informix already have OLAP capabilities. IBM's product will be based on Arbor's Essbase OLAP server and will support OLAP queries against data in DB2 databases. Microsoft is expected to release Plato, an OLAP server that will work with Sphinx, an upgraded SQL Server database. Both Plato and Sphinx will run on the Windows NT platform. Microsoft will also add OLAP capabilities to Excel and Visual Basic. For OLAP vendors, the emphasis this year will be integrating products with database and applications software, as well as delivering products that are easier to deploy, manage, and use.

Data-mining algorithms scan databases to uncover relationships or patterns. IBM will continue to introduce new data mining products and will commercialize text-mining software, which uses linguistic principles to scan and organize text. Applications of this technology include sorting through call-center records to find trends. NCR will integrate industry-specific data mining solutions with its products. In general, data mining tools are projected to become more available and easier to use.

Mattison, Rob. "Warehousing Wherewithal." *CIO* (April 1, 1996): 58-63.

The author states that no single vendor provides a turnkey approach to data warehousing because of the complexity of the technical, organizational, procedural, and operational issues involved. The majority of vendors focus on one of the three functional areas of a data warehouse and partner with vendors of products from other categories. The degree and quality of integration varies. The three areas are:

1. *Acquisition products*—Acquisition of data from legacy systems and outside sources. These products catalog (developing an inventory of where it is and what it means), clean/prepare (extracting from legacy files and reformatting), and transport data.

2. *Storage products*—Storage of data, which is managed by relational databases or specialized hardware/software, including symmetric multiprocessor (SMP) or massively parallel processor (MPP) machines. Relational databases typically run on Unix or mainframe platforms. When higher workloads are anticipated, SMP or MPP (very high end) machines are used.

3. *Access products*—User access, the widest range of products. These products fall into six categories:

   ▪ Intelligent agents and agencies. A business user asks the system to check on things, automatically send reports, and monitor the status of business functions.

   ▪ Query facilities and managed query environments.

   ▪ Statistical analysis.

   ▪ Data discovery. These tools use neural networks, fuzzy logic, decision trees, and other advanced mathematical and statistical techniques. The tools allow users to sift through massive amounts of raw data to discover interesting, insightful, and useful things.

   ▪ OLAP. Online analytical processing or multidimensional spreadsheet tools allow users to look at information from many different perspectives. These products dynamically slice and dice reports to look at different levels of the same information simultaneously.

■ Data visualization. These tools present data in compelling and easy-to-understand graphical representations.

The author cautions readers to scrutinize the product and service offerings of vendors to determine exactly what will be provided. The costs for a warehouse vary significantly, from $50,000 (leveraging existing hardware, software, and personnel) to millions. The hardware/software budget is allocated 60 percent to the storage component and 30 percent to data mining and user access technologies (10 percent is miscellaneous). The analysis and development budget is allocated 50 percent to building acquisition capabilities, 30 percent to developing user solutions, and 20 percent to creating databases in the storage component. Successful projects start as small, tightly defined systems designed to meet specific business needs.

Stedman, Craig. "Data Marts Move Front and Center." *Computerworld* (November 24, 1997): 63-64.

Because they are cheaper and easier to build than enterprise data warehouses, data marts are often built for individual business units. Organizations taking this approach risk ending up with disconnected data marts.

Vendors are now introducing products that let businesses build and centrally manage networks of compatible data marts. These products can, for example, provide for central staging of data to be fed into data marts so that each individual mart does not require its own link to production systems. Informatica Corp., with its Power-Center tool, and D2K, Inc., with Tapestry tools, are two such vendors.

Stedman, Craig. "Consolidation Wave Breaks Right for Users." *Computerworld* (November 17, 1997): 83, 86

Data warehousing vendors are merging; users benefit. "Building a data warehouse today is kind of like building your own Swiss watch," said Gene Alvarez, data warehousing administrator at 9West Group, Inc., in White Plains, New York. Fifty-five percent of sites are still writing their own programs to handle some pieces of back-end data preparation. Customers are getting more conservative; they don't want to buy tools from small companies and integrate them. A shakeout among vendors is going on.

Vijayan, Jaikumar. "NCR Broadens Data Warehouse Offerings." *Computerworld* (October 13, 1997): 14.

NCR will bundle SAS Institute's data analysis tools with NCR's data warehouse platforms. (NCR was one of the original data warehouse vendors and focused on the high-end market.) NCR is now attempting to broaden its appeal with a new low-end product. WorldMark 4700 (the low-end product starting at $158,000) supports up to 600 gigabytes, and WorldMark 5150 (the high-end product starting at $500,000) supports from 600 gigabytes to more than 100 terabytes. NCR is also working with Microsoft to port its Teradata engine to Windows NT.

Waltner, Charles. "Ready-Made Warehouses." *Information Week* (November 3, 1997): 100-108.

To save time and money, businesses—especially small and midsize businesses—are buying ready-made data warehouses, which are not as scalable or as flexible as custom solutions. The ready-made warehouses are designed for specific industries. Examples of problems common to a particular industry include customer retention for phone companies or fraud detection for credit card issuers. An example of a product is IBM's fraud and abuse management system (FAMS) for detecting false insurance claims.

The packaged products are the second generation of vertically oriented solutions. The first generation included data models, which reportedly failed because they were too generic. The packaged products reportedly halve the time and the cost to implement a warehouse, both of which help sell data warehousing to senior management. But packaged solutions can lack the flexibility needed for easy integration into an enterprise solution.

The article includes some results from Meta Group surveys. One chart reports "Average '97 Data Warehouse Budgets Across Industries." Telecom was the highest (about $4.75 million), and pharmaceuticals and process manufacturing was the lowest (about $1 million). The all-industries average was about $2 million. Another chart reports "How Data Warehouses Size Up Across Industries."

Telecom was the highest (about 300 gigabytes), and utilities and energy was the lowest (about 10 gigabytes). The all-industries average was about 100 gigabytes.

Weston, Randy. "SAP to Add Data Warehouse." *Computerworld* (June 16, 1997): 3.

SAP, one of the largest ERP software vendors, plans to embed data warehousing capabilities in its R/3 software. SAP's business customers will not have to build a separate data warehouse. Highlights of SAP's warehouse include:

- Preconfigured with R/3 business processes.
- Deployed as a central repository or at multiple locations.
- Includes a staging facility for automated data extraction and loading into the data warehouse from R/3 or other applications (including products from Oracle and Baan).

SAP predicts that its embedded functionality will cut time to build a data warehouse (18 to 36 months according to Meta Group) by 60 percent.

Wilson, Linda. "Industry-Specific Tools Emerging." *Computerworld* (December 15, 1997): 67, 70.

This article reports that vendors are developing data mining tools for specific industry segments. The mining engines are packaged with application-specific code, making the systems faster to implement. One vendor, HyperParallel, Inc., calls its application templates Solution Frameworks and its mining engine Discovery. HyperParallel, Inc., has templates for the retail industry (for functions such as markdown management), for banking (for functions such as fee tolerance), and for telecommunications. Other vendors developing niches include DataMind and Unica Technologies, Inc., for database marketing and Magnify, Inc., for fraud.

Even a large, technologically sophisticated organization, Bank of America, is evaluating HyperParallel's product for commercial banks. Bank of America reports that a template is a good place to start for customizing. Fleet Financial Group, Inc., plans to implement SAS Institute's Enterprise Miner and Exchange Applications, Inc.'s ValEx marketing campaign management tool. Using this combination, Fleet Financial Group projects a five-year ROI of 138 percent on a project investment of $30 million for a 70-person staff, data warehouse, and tools.

Web Sites

The Data Warehousing Knowledge Center, http://www.datawarehouse. org/

"The Data Warehousing Knowledge Center is a not-for-profit organization whose objective is to unite data warehousing users, vendors, consultants and other important parties into mutually beneficial relationships. The DWKC is completely independent of all data warehousing organizations and will remain an unbiased source of quality information about data warehousing technologies. The DWKC is a neutral organization that assembles and organizes information from many sources, and displays this information for its participants."

The Data Warehousing Information Center, http://pwp.starnetinc.com/ larryg/index.html

"This site's aim is to help readers learn about data warehousing and decision support systems. The site will:

- Provide links to vendors of tools for end-user data retrieval and analysis, tools for building and maintaining system infrastructure, and tools directed at specific industries and functions
- Point the reader to data warehouse and decision support publications: articles, white papers, books, technical evaluations, periodicals, and other non-vendor sources of information
- List service providers: consultants, trainers, conference and seminar organizers"

The Data Warehousing Institute, http://www.dw-institute.com/

"The Data Warehousing Institute achieves its mission through sharing information about the best practices and real world lessons of data warehousing professionals. Founded in 1995, TDWI sponsors and promotes a worldwide membership program, annual educational conferences, a seminar series, onsite educational courses, solution provider partnerships, awards programs for the best practices in data warehousing and innovative technologies, resourceful publications, in-depth research programs, and a comprehensive web site."

CIO's Data Warehousing Research Center, http://www.cio.com/forums/data/

"CIO has been covering data warehousing since information gathering of this type was just a gleam in someone's electric eye. While data warehousing is almost without exception a costly and time-consuming venture, the competitive advantage that superior business intelligence provides may be priceless. The site links to relevant articles, books, case studies, vendors, organizations, and a glossary."

Knowledge Discovery Nuggets, http://www.kdnuggets.com/

KD Nuggets "is a free newsletter on data mining and knowledge discovery topics."

Complete Intranet Resource—Intranet Reference Site, http://www.intrack.com/intranet/

"This site is your source to information on intranets. We will be providing visitors with resources that will help them research, plan, design and implement intranets. You could be a student researching intranets, a webmaster starting on an intranet project or just someone curious about the concept. This site will provide you with information that will give you a head start on your project. We will try and answer all your questions. Provide you with links to articles, case studies, software packages and more."

Other online sources of information about data warehousing and data mining include the Web sites of IT-oriented research organizations, such as the following:

- AMR, http://www.amr.com
- Forrester, http://www.forrester.com
- Gartner, http://gartner4.gartnerweb.com/public/static/home/home.html
- Giga, http://www.gigaweb.com

- Meta, http://www.metagroup.com/
- Also visit those of IT vendors and IT consulting firms (there is a charge for information on some of these sites)

Part 2. Other Relevant Literature

Related Technologies (DSS, EIS, etc.)

Ashton, Alison Hubbard, Robert H. Ashton, and Mary N. Davis. "White-Collar Robotics: Leveraging Managerial Decision Making." *California Management Review.* Vol. 37, no. 1 (Fall 1994): 83-109.

White-collar robotics refers to leveraging managers' efforts with managerial decision models. The authors argue that very simple decision models will improve managers' decisionmaking: While some models may need to be computerized, in many cases paper-and-pencil models will often make more accurate decisions than managers do. Their focus is on repetitive decisions (e.g., forecasting future revenues, evaluating loan applicants). Repetitive decisions are characterized by a larger experience base, more straightforward identification and measurement of relevant information, and easier definition of success and failure. The authors describe several straightforward approaches to improving managers' repetitive forecasts (regression models, managers' bootstrapping models, combinations of modeling and managers, composite forecasts of multiple managers) and show that all of them result in more accurate forecasts than those actually made by managers. However, managers offer many objections to using models. There is some evidence that managers are motivated to systematically bias (revenue) forecasts downward: Managers may not want their forecasting biases corrected.

Belcher, Lloyd W. "Assessing the Value of Conoco's EIS." *MIS Quarterly.* Vol. 17, no. 3 (September 1993): 239-253.

Organizations do not usually cost-justify EISs. Instead, executive sponsors who believe in a project simply provide the resources needed to start it. However, because the costs of maintaining EISs are considerable (over $200,000 per year, on average), EISs are very vulnerable to cost-cutting initiatives. Consequently, it makes sense to evaluate the benefits of the projects post hoc. This article describes an evaluation of the EIS at Conoco. The evaluation methodology was designed to identify users and their require- ments, eliminate low-value applications, identify applications to be enhanced or expanded, and produce a post-hoc cost/benefit analy- sis. Emphasis was placed on realistic measurement of quantifiable benefits coupled with an enumeration of intangibles.

Conoco found that benefits outweighed costs by about five to one. Fifteen percent of applications were identified as weak, and 90 per- cent of these were eliminated. A decision to enhance the consisten- cy of the look and feel of the applications was made. Ongoing evaluation was subsequently built into the application itself. The ar- ticle concludes with a set of lessons learned about EIS evaluation.

Schmitz, John D., Gordon D. Armstrong, and John D.C. Little. "Cover-Story—Automated News Finding in Marketing." *Interfaces.* Vol. 20, no. 6 (November-December 1990): 29-38.

This article describes the approach used by Ocean Spray Cranber- ries to manage the very large databases collected through bar-code scanners in supermarkets. Until the mid-1980s, Ocean Spray tracked the sales and share of its products with summary data pro- vided by companies like A.C. Nielsen, supplemented with data from Ocean Spray operations. By the mid-1980s, data suppliers were able to provide national samples from supermarkets with scanners. Because the amount of data involved is 100 to 1,000 times greater than that previously available, it is important to consider carefully how such data will be managed and analyzed.

Ocean Spray worked with Information Resources, Inc. (IRI) of Chicago to develop a strategy for handling data (also acquired from IRI). Ocean Spray operates with a lean staff, suggesting a strategy in which marketing users do most of their own retrieval and analy- sis supported by a very small support group (one marketing profes- sional plus the database administrators). The technology enables users to retrieve any fact from the database in a few steps, but most of the use of the data comes from standard reports. Use of the technology was uneven: It was little used in Sales, more widely used in Marketing. Even there, however, users believed that using the computer was not their job: They wanted preanalyzed reports. In addition to numerous standard reports, Ocean Spray adopted an expert system called CoverStory (developed by IRI) that produces summary memoranda describing the results of specific analyses of scanner data. The reports resemble those that a marketing analyst would write. They do not present model results directly, but rather report facts, such as share, volume, winners and losers, and factors that account for brand performance.

Todd, Peter, and Izak Benbasat. "An Experimental Investigation of the Impact of Computer Based Decision Aids on Decision Making Strategies." *Information Systems Research.* Vol. 2, no. 2 (June 1991): 87-115.

The authors proposed and demonstrated that specific features of a decision support system can alter the effort required to implement a particular decisionmaking strategy, and thus influence strategy selection. Their findings show that decisionmakers adopt search strategies that reduce the cognitive effort they have to expend. The authors conclude that designers and implementers of decision support systems should be quite concerned about whether decisionmakers are actually using DSS to maximize decision quality. They worry that some of the key influences on user behavior may be neither intended nor desirable.

Strategic Data Planning

Chandra, Rob, Mark Knickrehm, and Anthony Miller. "Healthcare's IT Mistake." *The McKinsey Quarterly.* No. 3 (1995): 91-100.

To succeed with IT, health care participants will have to avoid the pitfalls that have prevented their IT investments from paying off so far. The article focuses on four areas:

1. Focus on improving the productivity of front-line caregivers. Physicians have a real opportunity to use information to support the adoption of care giving standards or protocols.

2. Make IT investments in the right sequence. The sequence is:

   a. Integrate basic information (e.g., care data) across the business system (inpatient, laboratory, pharmacy) to create a complete picture of what was done to the patient, by whom, at what cost.

   b. Capture clinical data regarding outcomes such as recovery time.

   c. Gather longitudinal data.

3. Match your IT investments to the stage of market evolution (fee-for-service through restructured).

4. Improve your execution skills (e.g., IT systems must be linked to measures of physician performance and rewards).

Levitin, A.V., and T.C. Redman. "Data as Resource: Properties, Implications, and Prescriptions." *Sloan Management Review.* Vol. 40, no. 1 (Fall 1998): 89-101.

Data have many different properties from traditional resources; two components are data models and values. Models are definitions of entities, attributes, and relationships. Records are concrete, unlike models. They are physical manifestations of data in paper files, etc. The goal is to create a sufficient, but not excessive, supply of data; provide legitimate users with timely and efficient access; and protect from unplanned destruction and unauthorized access. Nine prescriptions for data management are given.

Shanks, Graeme. "The Challenges of Strategic Data Planning in Practice: An Interpretive Case Study." *Journal of Strategic Information Systems.* Vol. 6, no. 1 (March 1997): 69-90.

The article presents a case study of strategic data planning (SDP) in an Australian bank. As with many other industries, Australian banking suffered severe profit pressure and cost-cutting exercises in the early 1990s. The case-study bank had a decentralized organizational structure. Only for very large IS projects (greater than $1 million) was approval at the corporate level required. Each business unit had its own IS group. In the late 1980s, a centralized IS group was established for infrastructure, and a data planning initiative (with detailed data modeling) was undertaken. Then, in the early 1990s, data administration was sacrificed to cost cutting because it was seen as infrastructure and not directly involved in IS development. More recently, the bank has begun a data warehousing project.

Many objectives of SDP were not met (e.g., development of integrated systems and elimination of redundant data), but the concepts of data sharing and data as a corporate resource became well established in the bank. On the other hand, there was little understanding of data architecture and its potential organizational benefits. Use of the data architecture was countercultural in IS: Project teams had little incentive to use it. The architecture contained many cross-functional concepts with new terminology that were not understood, and training sessions were largely ineffective. The data architecture was subsequently used in the development of the data warehouse.

Among the conclusions were:

- The data architecture is difficult to understand and communicate.
- Sustaining management support for the data architecture is difficult.
- The data architecture is organizationally difficult to implement.
- SDP may not be the best way to build a data architecture.
- A balance between long-term and short-term benefits must be achieved.

Goodhue, Dale L., Laurie J. Kirsch, Judith A. Quillard, and Michael D. Wybo. "Strategic Data Planning: Lessons from the Field." *MIS Quarterly.* Vol. 16, no. 1 (March 1992): 11-34.

The literature argues that SDP (i.e., information engineering, as in IBM's BSP and Holland's IRM) is a valuable means to increase data integration in large organizations. However, empirical research has found more problems than success. The authors conducted detailed case studies and concluded that SDP is not the best planning approach in all situations. In addition, it may not be the best way to develop a data architecture given the time and cost requirement, the potential for errors, and the highly abstract results.

The data integration problem is believed to stem from the functionally oriented nature of traditional system development. Methods like information engineering assume that an organization's information needs involve a relatively stable group of data entities. SDP is a formal, top-down approach that builds a model of the enterprise, its functions and processes. It focuses on the organization's shared data and produces an information architecture. Five categories of potential outcomes have been claimed for SDP:

a. Implementation of integrated systems.

b. A data architecture (defined as a set of constraints on the system development process that ensures a desired level of data integration in all future development or maintenance activities).

c. Identification of applications priorities.

d. Rethinking business processes.

e. Communication and education.

Some researchers have focused on the pitfalls of SDP (e.g., an inadequate long-range perspective, lack of detail in the plan). These authors question the very appropriateness of SDP. Their study focused on planning efforts ranging from 10 weeks to one year long and from $450,000 to $1.9 million. They found that the outcomes achieved were not necessarily those aimed for. Among their conclusions about the method are the following: SDP assumes that all systems will be redesigned and actually starts the process of systems redesign. Thus, it is overkill in many instances. SDP fails when top managers are not committed to the goal of information sharing. SDP cannot succeed when IT governance is highly decentralized; further benefits require enforcement of the architecture, which is unlikely in this situation. SDP provides little value added when the organization already has common data definitions and codes for part numbers, etc. There is little consensus about the desirable form of the architecture SDP is supposed to produce. Further, the expense of SDP may not be required to produce such an architecture. Some gurus argue that the required architecture is generic enough to be stolen from other organizations rather than be built from scratch. SDP takes too long to bring novice modelers up the learning curve. SDP is an inefficient approach to identifying system priorities. The detail of SDP drowns creativity. Time requirements of the method lead to the selection of the wrong participants. The new understanding created by SDP is hard to communicate and does not justify the cost.

SDP is most appropriate when organizations plan to develop new integrated systems from scratch. More attention should be devoted to the question of precisely what an architecture for an organization consists of. Generalized or industry-specific architectures are a likely solution.

Harvey, Michael, Jonathan Palmer, and Cheri Speier. "Implementing Intra-Organizational Learning: A Phased-Model Approach Using Intranet Technology." *University of Oklahoma College of Business Administration Working Paper* (1997).

Information sharing in organizations is more a cultural problem than a technology problem. Nevertheless, organizations need common channels to communicate, such as an enterprise-wide intranet. This paper discusses the elements required in an organizational IT infrastructure to support organizational learning. Four cultural orientations toward information sharing have been identified:

1. Knowing culture—devoted to finding the best way to operate.

2. Understanding culture—guided by strong values which become a ruling myth.

3. Thinking culture—oriented toward problem finding and solving.

4. Learning culture—encourages experimentation, constructive dissent, and open discussion of failure.

The authors argue that different IT infrastructures facilitate different cultures. They propose a phase model for creating a learning culture. Phase 1 is to stimulate learning between management levels in the organization. Phase 2 is to expand the learning environment across functions. The technology link here is to give each functional unit its own distinctive view of shared information. Phase 3 is to encourage learning between divisions in the same organization, which necessitates addressing significant political barriers. The focus of efforts here should be to promote direct communications across divisions. Phase 4 is to bolster learning between organizations owned by a single company. Intranet development can support each phase in the process.

Meyer, Marc H., and Michael H. Zack. "The Design and Development of Information Products." *Sloan Management Review.* Vol. 37, no., 3 (Spring 1996): 43-59.

This article develops a framework derived from research and experience with physical products that can be applied to the architecture of information products. Different architectures result in different product functionality, cost, quality, and performance. The architecture of information products exhibits characteristics of both assembled and non-assembled physical products. The product platform of an information product is best viewed as a repository of information content and structure. The process platform of an information product is composed of five information processing stages: acquisition, refinement, storage/retrieval, distribution, and presentation or use. The flexibility to create numerous information product derivatives becomes the basis of a firm's ability to leverage its information assets.

Determining Information Requirements

Byrd, Terry Anthony, Kathy L. Cossick, and Robert W. Zmud. "A Synthesis of Research on Requirements Analysis and Knowledge Acquisition Techniques." *MIS Quarterly.* Vol. 16, no. 1 (March 1992): 117-138.

Developers of expert systems (ESs) have produced a body of literature about knowledge acquisition techniques that does not build on the extensive research on IS requirements analysis. The authors argue that the underlying processes of the two techniques are quite similar. As with IS, development of ESs is most successful with extensive user involvement. Both types of systems can either support or replace users. Further, ESs are increasingly becoming embedded in traditional IS. Finally, the same personnel more often perform both processes.

Leonard, Dorothy, and Jeffrey F. Rayport. "Spark Innovation Through Empathic Design." *Harvard Business Review.* Vol. 75, no. 6 (November-December 1997): 102-113.

Traditional requirements analysis techniques (interviews, focus groups, surveys, etc.) work for improving products that customers know well. But they don't work for designing new products that meet needs customers may not yet recognize. Empathic design techniques—gathering, analyzing, and applying information gleaned from observing customers using products and services in the context of their own environments—enable designers to go beyond improvements to familiar products. Through observation, designers can uncover both unexpected uses for their products and design flaws not identified in surveys.

The authors highlight some differences between inquiry and observation. Some of the drawbacks of inquiry are that people can't ask for something they don't know is technically possible; people are generally unreliable reporters of their own behavior; people tend to give answers they think are expected or desired; and people are less likely to recall their feelings about intangible characteristics of products when they aren't in the process of using them. However, sophisticated observers can see solutions to unarticulated needs.

Sharda, Ramesh, and David M. Steiger. "Inductive Model Analysis Systems: Enhancing Model Analysis in Decision Support Systems." *Information Systems Research.* Vol. 7, no. 3 (September 1996): 328-341.

This paper discusses the problem of model analysis, specifically the computer-aided analysis of multiple instances of the same model representing different historical situations and/or what-if cases posed by a decisionmaker. This problem is important because the true purpose of modeling is the process of developing understanding or insight into that which is modeled. Insight into the situation modeled does not always develop easily when there are many interacting components in the model.

Current model analysis systems differ in the type of processing logic used: deductive, statistical reasoning, or inductive. Deductive model analysis systems address questions such as "Why is this the solution to the model?" They are limited to a single modeling paradigm or problem domain, and most implementations are limited to analyzing one model instance at a time. Statistical inference systems produce summary statistics of a model's output variables but do not address other analysis questions, such as "Which parameter has the greatest impact on the model's output?"

The authors believe that the greatest potential lies in inductive model analysis systems, which operate on a set of related model instances (e.g., different historical situations or what-if cases). The goal of these analysis operations is to assist the user in analyzing various model instances, thereby producing insight into the underlying decision-making environment. The authors describe in detail a prototype inductive model analysis system, called INSIGHT.

Trice, Andrew, and Randall Davis. "Heuristics for Reconciling Independent Knowledge Bases." *Information Systems Research.* Vol. 4, no. 3 (September 1993): 262-288.

The task of identifying discrepancies between independent bodies of knowledge is an inevitable part of any large knowledge acquisition effort.

Watson, Hugh J., and Mark N. Frolick. "Determining Information Requirements for an EIS." *MIS Quarterly.* Vol. 17, no. 3 (September 1993): 255-269.

EIS is a term used to refer to software for accessing news; stock prices; and information about competitors and customers, etc. (Today, the capabilities provided by an EIS would often be provided through a corporate intranet. Thus, some of the article's findings will apply to intranets.) The development of an EIS is viewed as a high-risk project, since one study found a 40 percent failure rate. Reasons for failure include user unfamiliarity with computer systems and IS specialists' lack of understanding of executive work. Accurate requirements determination is a major problem. There are reasons to believe that requirements elicitation techniques should be tailored to particular problem domains.

Information requirements can be specified at two levels of analysis: organization (e.g., overall IS structure for the organization, including applications and databases) and application (needs for a particular application such as an EIS). Many commonly used information requirements elicitation techniques are problematic for EIS; some may be useful only for initial development, others only for ongoing development. The authors surveyed EIS developers about the frequency of use and usefulness of various requirements analysis techniques.

Among the findings are the following: Discussions were conducted with executives only 62 percent of the time during initial EIS development. (The authors considered this finding troublesome.) Executives were frequently described as unwilling to spend time discussing their requirements. IS specialist knowledge of the business is critical in gaining time with executives. Discussions with executives' support personnel is a good surrogate for discussions with executives for information gathering (though not for relationship development/credibility enhancement). When executives volunteer requirements for EIS, they sometimes identify indicators that are most useful at making the executives' units look good. Although the literature claims that the critical success factors technique is likely to be essential to successful EIS development, only 40 percent of the surveyed organizations used this technique. Strategic business objectives (requiring a cross-functional look at the business) are a potentially useful complement to the critical success factors technique. The most highly rated technique was developer attendance at relevant business meetings. It was also quite useful for developers to study the organization's strategic plans.

Meyer, Marc H., and Michael H. Zack. "The Design and Development of Information Products." *Sloan Management Review.* Vol. 37, no. 3 (Spring 1996): 43-59.

Companies that produce information in printed or electronic form can learn much from research on physical products. The focus of this article is on the development of product and process platforms for information products. A framework is provided and applied to two firms that are creating competitive advantage by refining information for customers.

Individual and Organizational Learning, Knowledge Discovery

Cowan, David A. "Developing a Process Model of Problem Recognition." *Academy of Management Review.* Vol. 11, no. 4 (October 1986): 763-776.

This article focuses on the formulation phase of the problem-solving process at the individual level of analysis, which has generally been underresearched. The focus on problem situations is warranted by the fact that problem situations are believed to be more frequent than opportunity or crisis situations and are believed to have different triggers. Opportunities tend to be triggered by a single idea; crises by a single, immediate and important triggering event. By contrast, problems generally require multiple stimuli and milder pressures than crises. And, in problem situations, decisionmakers appear to desire a better understanding of the situation before they act.

Not all problems are identified in the same way: Some are automatic, based on prior experience; others require focused search and evaluation of more information. Problem recognition has three general stages: gestation/latency, categorization (awareness that something is wrong but not being able to explain what the problem is), and diagnosis (greater certainty of problem description). Seven process variables represent the individual's actual process of problem recognition: scanning, arousal, clarification, classification, information search, inference, and problem description. Factors that may affect problem recognition are cue discrepancy, perceived urgency to respond, persistence or accumulation of discrepancies, familiarity, priority, and availability of information.

Schoemaker, Paul J. H., and J. Edward Russo. "A Pyramid of Decision Approaches." *California Management Review.* Vol. 36, no. 1 (Fall 1993): 9-31.

Most managers still make decisions based on intuition. Decision research has revealed two common flaws in intuitive decisionmaking: random inconsistency and systematic distortion. Decisions based on rules are somewhat more accurate than wholly intuitive ones. However, industry and occupation specific rules are vulnerable to environmental changes. Generic rules also have problems. The dictionary rule (one criterion at a time) gives enormous importance to the first attribute (and therefore makes sense only when there is a dominant attribute). The threshold rule (only if all preset criteria are met) is too unforgiving. Importance weightings allow one to develop a model. Weightings can be determined directly or inferred. Bootstrapping is replacing the decisionmaking by a model of factors and weights derived from the decisionmaker. Value analysis goes beyond lists of factors to uncover the true values of the decisionmaker by linking the factors to key objectives. Different techniques result in different decisions for the same problem.

Vandenbosch, Betty, and Chris Higgins. "Information Acquisition and Mental Models: An Investigation into the Relationship between Behavior and Learning." *Information Systems Research.* Vol. 7, no. 2 (June 1996): 198-214.

This article addresses the problem of executive use of decision systems: Despite many reports of their success, more than half of executives surveyed did not believe their organizations were getting the most from their IT investments. Further, other researchers identified 20 ways in which executive support systems can fail. The authors contend that such systems fail because executives do not learn from them, that is, change their behavior as a result of information processing.

The two components of learning are maintaining mental models and building new ones. Executive support systems should be designed to encourage mental model building. Information can be acquired in two ways: scanning (browsing without a problem to solve) and focused search (for specific information). Scanning is particularly important to senior executives. But typical information systems are built with focused search in mind. The authors believe that scanning can enable mental model formation as well as maintenance but that focused search enables mental model maintenance.

The empirical research supported the research model. Systems tend to support model maintenance rather than building. Without an explicit focus on using systems to support model development, learning is unlikely to happen.

Small Businesses and IT

Cragg, Paul B., and Malcolm King. "Small-Firm Computing: Motivators and Inhibitors." *MIS Quarterly.* Vol. 17, no. 1 (March 1993): 47-60.

New applications (after the initial setting up of a computer system) were introduced in firms where the owner was enthusiastic about IT but not in firms where the owner was not enthusiastic. Discouraging factors include the lack of training. Training was confined to the initial setup period and limited to the hands-on users. The training was highly specific to the applications installed. This discouraged consideration of new applications or enhancements to existing applications. Managerial time was a big constraint. Prior installations were very time consuming and discouraged upgrades. Weak financial position was also a factor that discouraged additional investment. Small firms are very dependent on good vendor support.

d'Amboise, Gerald, and Marie Muldowney. "Management Theory for Small Business: Attempts and Requirements." *Academy of Management Review.* Vol. 13, no. 2 (April 1988): 226-240.

A small business is defined as one that is independently owned and operated and that is not dominant in its field of operation. It is generally considered to employ no more than 500 people and to have sales of less than $20 million. This article addresses small and medium-sized businesses.

Small firms can be distinguished from large ones by the diffuseness of interaction among departments, which permits easy access to information required to respond to task demands but induces many emotional interdependencies that impede resolution of interdepartmental conflict. Often the goals of the small businessperson are vague, poorly defined, pragmatic and short range. For the manager of the small business, "the rational model [of decisionmaking] seems to be much too ambitious an undertaking. The principal concern of the small business is cash flow.

DeLeone, W. "Determinants of Success for Computer Usage in Small Business." *MIS Quarterly.* Vol. 12, no. 1 (March 1988): 51-61.

The author surveyed 93 manufacturing firms in Los Angeles, with an average of 62 employees and $5 million annual revenue. Chief executive knowledge of computers and involvement in IS operations was positively associated with IS success. Neither use of external programming support nor level of employee computer training was associated with IS success.

Fuller, T. "Fulfilling IT Needs in Small Businesses: A Recursive Learning Model." *International Small Business Journal.* Vol. 14, no. 4 (July-September 1996): 25-44.

Fuller's central thesis is that barriers to IT development in small businesses center around three issues: (a) the structure of the IT sector, (b) relationships among actors (including management, vendors, suppliers, and consultants) in the IT adoption process, and (c) the lack of skills and knowledge of these actors. Fuller identifies three areas of necessary learning about IT: (a) learning to make optimal use of the system, (b) learning the know-how contained in the software, and (c) learning to adopt the tools to be more effective in the organizational context.

The model of development and adoption proposed is a process model, a holistic picture meant to assist with identification of inefficiencies in the overall process of technology transfer. Elements of the model are clients' perceived needs, design and development, provision, absorption, and the relationships among the key actors in each stage. Key competencies of actors in the model are to reduce the gaps between supply and demand created by information asymmetry and by technological complexity, and to manage the change resulting from innovation.

There are two significant implications, in Fuller's view. First, information asymmetry between the IT industry and small business threatens potential development of this sector (small businesses have little to no direct contact with system designers). Second, the goal is demand pull rather than supply push. In response, Fuller puts forth two recommendations. First, provide suppliers with incentives for meeting the needs of small businesses. Second, build into publicly financed interventions in small business development (publications, programs) education regarding the integration of IT with business issues.

Lees, J.D. "Successful Development of Small Business Information Systems." *Journal of Systems Management.* Vol. 25, no. 3 (September 1987): 32-39.

Evidently using same the data set as Lees and Lees (1987), this study goes into further detail about success factors and benefit attainment for small business IS. Respondents were individuals responsible for purchasing decisions in 56 U.S. small businesses using microcomputers. Success was measured by usage and satisfaction. Those converting all applications at once more were successful, especially regarding usage. Success decreased when management was not involved in system selection.

The use of consultants for training was positively associated with success. The use of consultants for information needs assessment, hardware or software selection, or system modification were all negatively associated with success.

The use of vendors for training, software modification, repairs, and maintenance was positively associated with success. The use of vendors for hardware or software selection was negatively associated with success and achieving IT benefits. There was a high positive association between a good vendor relationship and decisionmaker satisfaction.

Lees, J.D., and D.D. Lees. "Realities of Small Business Information System Implementation." *Journal of Systems Management.* Vol. 25, no. 1 (January 1987): 6-13.

This article provides descriptive data based on a survey of small organizations (69 percent with fewer than 20 employees). The major implementation goal was to improve operational procedures. Foremost among anticipated benefits (which were largely realized) were better record keeping; the availability of more timely, accurate, and expanded information; improved customer service; increased productivity; and enhanced management control and decisionmaking. Criteria for vendor selection included reputation, business and technical skills, availability of training, and availability of integrated hardware/software packages. The impact of vendors and consultants on successful implementation was overestimated.

Thong, J.Y.L., C.S. Yap, and K.S. Raman. "Engagement of External Expertise in Information Systems Implementation." *Journal of Management Information Systems.* Vol. 11, no. 2 (Fall 1994): 209-231.

The authors surveyed and interviewed project managers (often the CEO) and user-managers in 57 small businesses in Singapore. They examined differences between two strategies: the consultant-vendor approach, in which consultants (for requirements and analysis and implementation assistance) are retained separately from vendors (for providing hardware and software solutions); and the vendor-only approach, in which the vendor performed all of the functions of consultants in addition to selling the system. Compared with the consultant-vendor approach, the vendor-only approach was associated with more satisfied users, higher organizational impact (manifested by decreased operating cost), more effective information systems, and better vendor support (in terms of adequacy of technical support during implementation, quality of technical support, quality of training, and relationships with other parties in the project). No significant differences were found between the two groups in terms of system usage, total application impact (though there was a difference in average application impact), and effectiveness of consultancy services.

Thong, James Y.L., Chee-Sing Yap, and K.S. Raman. "Top Management Support, External Expertise and Information Systems Implementation in Small Businesses." *Information Systems Research.* Vol. 7, no. 2 (June 1996): 248-267.

Small businesses face substantially greater risks in IT implementation than larger businesses as a result of several characteristics of small businesses. Small businesses have simple and highly centralized structures, with the chief executive making most of the critical decisions. They also tend to employ generalists rather than specialists. Operating procedures are rarely written down or standardized. They rarely use management techniques such as financial analysis. They may also suffer from resource constraints.

This study examined the effects of top management support (a critical success factor in IT implementation in large organizations), external consultants, and vendor support. Results show that top management support is not as important as effective external IS expertise (vendor support) in small business IS implementation. High-quality external IS expertise is particularly important for small businesses suffering from severe resource constraints.

Yap, C.S., C.P. P. Soh, and K.S. Raman. "Information Systems Success Factors in Small Business." *Omega International Journal of Management Science.* Vol. 20, no. 5/6 (September-November 1992): 597-609.

Using the same data set as Soh, Yap, and Raman (1992), the authors take a broader look at IS success factors in 96 small businesses in Singapore. Success is positively correlated with (in rank order of strength of correlation) consultant effectiveness, vendor support, firm financial resources, firm computer experience, user participation in implementation, and CEO support in implementation. No correlation was found between success and either the presence of an IS professional on staff or the number of administrative computer applications. An interesting additional analysis showed a positive association between success and the number of financial and accounting applications.

Case-Study Protocol

Background of Case-Study Company

Purpose:

Describes the industry and the case-study company. This section provides essential background about the company, including relative size, relevant strategic challenges, resources of the IS or IT function, key management personnel, organization structure, and controls infrastructure.

Potential Sources of Information:

Public information such as the annual report and newspaper articles, internal company documents, the primary site contact person, and other senior executives.

Data Warehousing History at Study Site

Purpose:

Describes when, why, and how data warehousing got started at the case-study organization.

Potential Sources of Information:

The primary site contact person; the data warehouse project manager(s) and project sponsor(s); key business unit managers/users; and internal company documents.

Typical Questions:

Initial effort

- In what business unit did the initial data warehousing/data mining effort originate? When?

- What was the business opportunity or problem that led to the effort?

- Why was the data warehouse/data mine viewed as a solution to the opportunity or problem?

- Briefly, what was the state of the IT infrastructure and IT governance at that time?

- Briefly, what prior efforts had been undertaken in EISs or related technologies?

- What are/were the outcomes of the data warehouse/data mine project?

Subsequent efforts

- Have other data warehouse/data mine projects been undertaken since the initial effort?

- What is the overall architecture of these efforts?

  - enterprise data warehouse

  - dependent data mart(s)

  - stand-alone data mart(s) (If so, is the intent to evolve to an enterprise warehouse? Why or why not?)

- What is the overall governance of these efforts?

- What is the current status of these projects?

- What additional efforts are planned?

- What business results, if any, have been obtained?

- What problems, if any, have been encountered?

Focal initiative

- To be decided in collaboration with study site:
    - On what data warehouse/data mine initiative should this research project focus?
    - Why?
- What is the relationship of this project to other data warehouse/data mine initiatives?

Focal Data Warehousing Project

Purpose:

Describes in more detail the specific data warehouse/data mine initiative on which this research project focuses.

Potential Sources of Information:

The primary site contact person, other senior executives; the data warehouse project manager(s), and project sponsor(s); key business unit managers whose organizations use the warehouse; analysts who use the warehouse; and representatives from IT, finance, internal audit, and human resources.

Typical Questions:

Background

- Describe the business unit and business problem or opportunity.
- Who initiated the effort?
- Was the IS department involved, and if so how?
- What was the role of the champion of the project?
- How was funding obtained?

- Is there any organized program of knowledge management, organizational learning, or intellectual capital in the organization? And how does the current data warehousing/data mining project relate?

Data warehousing/data mining project

- Was the effort structured as a formal project?

- If so, who are the project manager and team members, what are the key milestones, and what are the details of project justification and budgeting?

- Were the project manager and team members assigned to work on the project full time?

- What other people were involved in the project, and what were their roles?

  - External consultants?

  - Vendors?

  - Business unit representatives?

  - IS specialists?

- What were the roles initially envisioned for these project participants?

- What effect has personnel turnover had on the project?

- What organizational issues arose during the effort?

  - Data quality?

  - Data ownership?

  - Data access?

- What difficulties were there in agreeing on contents, usage, naming conventions?

  - Other?

- How were these difficulties addressed?

Architectural, technical, and support decisions

- What architecture did your organization choose—data warehouse or data mine (which type)?

  - Why was this architecture chosen?

  - How was this decision made?

  - Has the initial decision changed over time? If so, why?

- Was the planning top down (data warehouse first) or bottom up (data mine first)? Why?

- Was the implementation top down or bottom up? Why?

- What vendor, products, and services were selected? How, and why? What features were important in the selection?

  - What features were important six months after implementation?

  - What is your level of satisfaction with technical performance and vendor support?

- Was a generic data model used? If so, which one?

  - How satisfied were you with it?

- Is your data warehouse/data mine physically centralized or decentralized?

- Is your data warehouse/data mine logically centralized or decentralized?

- Who is responsible for data scrubbing and cleaning? For loading?

- Who is responsible for ongoing maintenance of the data warehouse/data mine?

  - What has been the nature of the "handoff" from data warehouse/data mine development to ongoing support?

- What are the current and planned linkages between the data warehouse/data mine and the intranet?

Data Warehouse/Data Mine Contents and Data Mining Tools

- What is in (and planned for) the data warehouse/data mine?
  - Legacy data?
  - External data?
  - Technical meta-data?
  - Business meta-data?
  - Video, multimedia?
- What is its current size and growth rate?
- What tools and techniques are supported (and planned) for data mining and data visualization?

Data Warehouse/Data Mine Users and Uses

- What business units use the data warehouse/data mine?
- How (for what types of analysis) do they use the data warehouse/data mine?
- At what level are the users?
  - Chauffeur-driven?
  - Point and click?
  - Power users?
- What are the profiles of the different categories of users?
- How has the user population grown?
- If the growth has been substantial, why? If not, why not?
- What effect has personnel turnover had on the data warehouse effort?
- Is data mining done? If so, by whom?

Training and Help

- What type of user training is provided? What levels of training (beginning, intermediate, and advanced)?

- What training is provided by the vendor(s)?

- What training is provided on site? How many days?

- Is a help desk function provided? If so, by whom?

- If data mining is done, how are data miners selected and trained?

- To what extent have spurious data mining results been a problem, and how is this problem addressed?

- To what extent has the difficulty of doing SQL analyses been a problem?

Internal Controls

- Who "owns" the data in the data warehouse/data mine?

- Who gets access to the data?

- How is access granted?

- Is access ever revoked?

Business Results

- What have been the business results?

- How have or will the benefits of the technology be measured?

- What were/are the dimensions of success?

- What external events affected (favorably or unfavorably) the success of the project?

- What functionality was anticipated? What was delivered?

- How do the actual costs compare to the initial estimates?

- Were initial budget estimates (time and cost) accurate?

- What key categories of expense are currently tracked?

- What are the performance measures?

- How are proposed new data acquisition or mining initiatives evaluated?

- To what extent has the data warehouse/data mine replaced earlier systems or technologies (e.g., EIS) and what benefits have accrued as a result?

- What was the level of participation by senior management?

- To what degree has data warehousing been integrated into the overall business strategy?

Lessons Learned

- What did you do right? Why?

- What would you change if you were starting over again? Why?

- How would you change?

Overall Evaluation of the Case

Purpose:

Describes and addresses some additional managerial issues that may be helpful to other organizations that are thinking about or embarking on data warehouse/data mine initiatives.

Potential Sources of Information:

The primary site contact person; other senior executives; the data warehouse project manager(s) and project sponsor(s); key business unit managers whose organizations use the warehouse; analysts who use the warehouse; and representatives from IT, finance, internal audit, and human resources.

Typical Questions:

Key Risks and Risk-Control Measures

- What were the key risks?
  - Project initiation risks?
  - Technology acquisition and development risks?
  - Data use and mining risks?
  - Other operational risks?
  - Customer or public perception risk?
  - Other competitive risks?
- What risk-control measures were employed?
  - Idea testing?
  - Project management?
  - Security and reliability?
  - Training?
  - Monitoring nature and level of use and user skill?
  - External communication?
  - Others?
- How effective were these measures?

Other Important Issues

- What are the high payoff uses of the data warehouse/data mine?
- What is the effect of the IT governance model on the data warehouse/data mine success?
- What have been the impacts of architectural and technical decisions?

- What light does this study shed on the data warehouse/data mine controversy?

- How important are technology product and service quality and quality of vendor support?

- What estimate of time to benefit in data warehouse/data mine projects does this study support?

- What is the relationship between the data warehouse/data mine and other organizational learning efforts?

- To what degree does the data warehouse/data mine displace older systems and technologies, and how much benefit results?

- To what degree is satisfactory resolution of political issues (e.g, regarding data access and use) essential to project success?

- What is the degree to which end users (vs. sophisticated analysts) actually use the data warehouse/data mine, and how important is it?

- To what degree is the relationship between IS/IT and the business units an issue in data warehouse/data mine strategy and success?

Glossary

Canned Reports—Canned reports are preformatted reports that are produced periodically or on demand when selected from a menu of available reports.

Data Access—Data access refers to the tools and techniques used to retrieve data stored in a database. Users construct requests for data or reports using a query language or by selecting from a menu.

Data Acquisition—Data for a data warehouse can be acquired from multiple sources—both internal and external to the business entity. Internal sources include online transaction processing systems and legacy systems. External sources include vendors who sell data (e.g., industry data or demographic data). Extraction and cleansing requirements may vary greatly.

Data Cleansing/Scrubbing—Data warehouses are typically assembled to support decision-oriented management queries. Answers to these management queries are only as accurate as the data in the warehouse. Data should be cleansed or scrubbed before being put in a warehouse. For example, a single customer, John J. Jones, could appear as John Jones, J. Jones, John J. Jones, Jack Jones, etc. Sophisticated data cleansing software may be required in addition to manual effort to identify and correct such multiple entries or errors in the source data.

Data Mart—A data mart is a collection of data and tools focused on a specific business unit or problem. Size does not distinguish data marts, but they tend to be smaller than data warehouses.

Data Mining—Data mining refers to a collection of tools and techniques used for inductive rather than deductive analyses. Using sophisticated data mining tools, analysts can explore detailed data and business transactions to uncover meaningful insights, relationships, trends, or patterns within the business activity and/or history. Data mining is used to identify hypotheses; traditional queries are used to test hypotheses.

Data Source—A data source is the point of origin for a particular piece of information. The data sources for a data warehouse could include multiple internal systems and external data vendors.

Data Storage—Data storage refers to the tools that load data into storage and the devices that provide an economical means to accumulate and store massive amounts of data generated by online transaction processing systems (e.g., point-of-sale, automated teller machines, reservation systems, customer service).

Data Warehouse—A data warehouse is an environment—not a single technology—comprising a data store and multiple software products, often obtained from different vendors. The products include tools for data extraction, loading, storage, access, query, and reporting. The data store is a collection of subject-oriented, integrated, time-variant, nonvolatile data, which are queried to support management decision making. Data stores include immense volumes of information detailing every aspect of a particular subject (such as customers, suppliers, products, markets, or quality). This information is drawn from a company's internal operational systems (such as order entry, sales, accounting, manufacturing, and human resources systems) and from external sources (such as purchased market research and demographic data). Data warehouses are typically assembled to support decision-oriented management queries. Because frequent and/or sophisticated queries can slow operational systems, data warehouses are established and maintained apart from the production systems. Cross-indexed and supported by significant computing power, data are refreshed on a periodic basis and do not change with each query or access.

Decision Support System—Decision support systems (DSSs) are designed to aid in specific decision-making tasks. DSSs include data, models, and easy-to-use interfaces that allow users to focus on particular decisions. DSSs are often implemented using spreadsheet packages, but more sophisticated technologies are available.

Enterprise Resource Planning—Enterprise resource planning (ERP) systems are complex suites of software packages that integrate applications for all functional areas of a business.

Executive Information System—Executive information systems (EISs) typically provide point-and-click access to data of interest to business executives.

Information Technology/Information Systems/Management Information Systems—The terms information technology (IT), information systems (IS), and management information systems (MIS) are often used interchangeably. These terms refer to hardware and software (e.g., the IT infrastructure is adequate for corporate expansion) and to the department or organization that provides systems solutions and support (e.g., MIS is responsible for vendor selection).

Knowledge Discovery in Databases—Knowledge discovery in databases (KDD) refers to discovering or finding new and meaningful patterns in data rather than verifying previous hypotheses.

Legacy Data—Packaged ERP systems typically replace multiple legacy systems—older software applications that may have been custom developed in-house. The data that reside in these older systems are referred to as legacy data. Legacy data can be made available to users by loading them into a data warehouse.

Meta Data—Meta data (data about data) describe the characteristics of data. For example, meta data might include specific details on the length, format, and definition of a particular field.

Online Analytical Processing—Online analytical processing (OLAP) includes decision-support software tools that let users analyze information summarized into multidimensional views or cubes. Two basic versions of online analytical processing are multidimensional online analytical processing (MOLAP) and relational online analytical processing (ROLAP). MOLAP systems are optimized for speed and ease of query response. ROLAP systems employ a table structure and can be scaled for very large databases.

Operational Data—Operational data typically originate in online transaction processing systems, which track day-to-day operations such as each sale, purchase, or inventory change. Online transaction processing systems are not well suited to answering questions that address the past, present, and future directions for a business (e.g., What are the trends of sales to customers in a particular state or city? What are the historical trends in unit costs?).

Operational Data Store—An operational data store includes some of the data extracted and summarized from online transaction processing systems. Information in an operational data store is updated on an ad hoc basis to reflect changes in the underlying transaction processing systems. (Note that information in a data warehouse is updated on a scheduled basis.) The purpose of an operational data store is to provide an operational query system without affecting the performance of the online transaction processing systems.

Query—A query is a user-initiated request for data or analyses/reports.

Relational Database—A relational database employs an organizational method that links information according to relationships such as account numbers and names.

SQL—Structured query language (SQL) is used by highly trained analysts for constructing database queries. SQL can be difficult and error-prone for complex queries. Users need to be familiar with the structure of the underlying data and with the syntax requirements of SQL statements.

Summary Data—Data warehouses can include raw data and summarized or aggregated data; the latter are often more useful in answering management queries. The aggregation process combines data into useful metrics for analysis. For example, raw data could include detailed orders by customer. Summary data could include sales by product family.

Transactional Data—Transactional data include raw details of every transaction recorded by an online transaction processing system. See *operational data*.

About the Authors

Barbara J. Bashein, Ph.D., is associate professor of information systems in the College of Business Administration at California State University San Marcos and adjunct professor of information science at Claremont Graduate University. She currently serves as the interim chief advancement officer at California State University San Marcos. Her research projects have been commissioned by the Financial Executives Research Foundation and the Society for Information Management. Dr. Bashein has over 25 years of business experience managing information systems organizations and projects. She was a partner with Andersen Consulting, where she directed and managed large-scale information systems and operations improvement projects in a variety of industries. Her other employment experience includes 10 years at Citicorp subsidiaries managing systems projects and two years at The RAND Corporation working on classified projects. She has conducted seminars and given presentations for many businesses and professional organizations on topics in information technology, project management, and change management.

M. Lynne Markus, Ph.D., is professor of management and information science at the Peter F. Drucker Graduate School of Management, Claremont Graduate University. Her research focuses on the role of information and communication technology in organizational design, performance, and change. Before joining the Drucker School, Dr. Markus was a member of the faculties of the Anderson Graduate School of Management (UCLA) and the Sloan School of Management (MIT). She has also taught at the Nanyang Business School, Singapore (as Shaw Foundation Professor) and Universidade Tecnica de Lisboa, Portugal (as Fulbright/FLAD Chair in Information Systems). Dr. Markus has received research grants and contracts from the National Science Foundation, the Office of Technology Assessment (U.S. Congress), The Advanced Practices Council of SIM International, the

Financial Executives Research Foundation, and Baan Institute. She is the author of three books and numerous articles in journals such as *MIS Quarterly, Management Science, Organization Science, Communications of the ACM*, and *Sloan Management Review.* She also serves on the editorial boards of several leading journals in the information systems field.

Acknowledgments

We gratefully acknowledge the support and help of the following individuals: the members of our Advisory Committee—Dan Bryce, Lawrence Davenport, Phil Greth, Mark Jacobson, and Dewey Norton; our chief contacts at the case-study companies—Dan Bryce at MSC.Software, Phil Greth at Cardinal Health, John Helmerci at Kraft Foods, and John Scholl at ALARIS Medical; and the professionals at the Financial Executives Research Foundation—Bob Colson, Rhona Ferling, Jim Lewis, and Cynthia Waller Vallario. We also thank all the people we interviewed, whether or not they were named in this report, for their time and thoughtful comments.